Wieniawski

Wladyslaw Duleba

Translated by Grazyna Czerny

PAGANINIANA PUBLICATIONS, INC.
211 West Sylvania Avenue, Neptune City, New Jersey 07753

Contents

Henryk Wieniawski.

Introduction

Undoubtedly Henryk Wieniawski was, as we see it now, one of the foremost violin virtuosos of the 19th-century "belle époque." His contemporaries unanimously acknowledged his marvellous technique, praised his uncommon musicality, and described his playing as ravishing, passionate, and almost demoniacal. They found him a match for the sparkling genius of Liszt. For all the customarily lavish language of the period, the critics' enthusiasm is evidence of Wieniawski's immense talent. The private life of the eminent violinist remains little known, and, in searching for facts, we find ourselves lost among irrelevant records or vague hints. Nevertheless, some evidence may be found which challenges the firmly-entrenched (though sketchy) image of the virtuoso. The range and intensity of his concert tours have always made it very difficult to trace all the significant moments of his life in Europe or in America. Julian Wieniawski-Jordan supplied the following excuse in his memoirs published in 1911: "Being too busy and having only scarce information, very much to my regret I am unable to provide a more extensive biography of my brother Henryk." As time elapsed, the matter became even more difficult. Special tribute must be paid to professor Jozef Reiss, the author of a complete monograph on Wieniawski, the sole work of this sort in Polish musical literature. For all its emotion-filled tenor, which frequently led the writer to subjective or extreme conclusions and appraisal, the book's wealth of information certainly deserves acknowledgement and appreciation. First published in 1931, it was reprinted in 1963; one can believe that no one else has endeavored to deal with the subject and study it in conformity with present-day musicological methods. Essays on Wieniawski can be found in specialized magazines, yet they merely supplement Reiss's work. Blank spots are numerous both in the virtuoso's bibliography and in the catalogs of those compositions of his which used to be very popular, especially when performed by the composer, yet are hardly indicative of his magnificent musicianship.

In fact, there is not a single complete and trustworthy catalog of

A youthful Henryk Wieniawski.

Wieniawski compositions with reliable dates of composition and publication. His brilliant career—one very representative of his time—has inspired the author of this book to follow the virtuoso's steps and take a close look at his epoch, in order to make of this book a magic lantern which uses the figure and career of Wieniawski as a transparency through which to project the musical life and atmosphere of those days. Certainly, the facts presented do not have bearing on the mainstream of the intellectual life of the period, yet the author found them sufficiently colorful, interesting, and characteristic of those days, to be included in this biography of the master of the bow. The diversified structure of the story is intended to meet the particular interests of the reader, and its style and movement make it like a motion picture. The aforementioned monograph by Professor Reiss has been assigned the role of travel guide on our trip to the nineteenth-century musical world. The author of the present volume has been quite persistent in compiling press notices and reviews, the main source for which was the *Revue et Gazette Musicale*, a French periodical of Wieniawski's time, which enjoyed a good reputation and kept track of contemporary musical events. To make the information even more complete, the author frequently quotes press news and notices from places which Wieniawski toured, as well as major articles and interesting reviews from the Polish press. The reader well acquainted with all kinds of literature on Wieniawski may encounter here a lot of facts and information differing from what may be found in the other sources. The data were sifted by juxtaposing excerpts of the Reiss monograph or Jordan's memoirs with official documents, and by reference to records once believed to be lost. The book also contributes to filling in some of the blank spots in the biography. Most of the illustrations have never been published before. The book is itself a kind of document, because, being by its very nature a product of the subjective choice of facts and sources, it appears to be a record of selected aspects of those days. Sometimes the writer smiles sardonically while examining a question or a case, in order to make the reader feel as if he were looking at a curved mirror's reflection of a fact or a character (e.g., the treatment of the famous *Carnaval russe* or Wieniawski's stay at the Voislins). Undoubtedly, drawing on documentary sources to reconstruct a past event includes the risk of erroneous interpretation, since it is hardly possible to find out to what extent the available press information is accurate and reliable. A great deal of contradiction among the news and information published long after an occurrence also causes difficulties in verifying the unsystematic and barely reliable records of Wieniawski's life. On the other hand, such a manner of exploring the past provides the reader with the flavor of authenticity.

A blustery Paris street-scene.

Wieniawski as a boy.

A Virtuoso's Life

Henryk Wieniawski was born in Lublin on the 10th of July in the year 1835.

His father, Tadeusz Wieniawski (1798-1889), "Master of philosophy, medicine, and surgery,"[1] joined the November Uprising as staff doctor for the 4th regiment of rifles. After the Uprising was crushed he spent some time abroad. Having returned from exile, he began medical practice in the town of Lublin.

Mrs. Regina Wieniawski, Henryk's mother, allegedly disinherited for her marriage,[2] was the daughter of a well-known Warsaw doctor, Jozef Wolff. Her brothers were Edward, an esteemed pianist and composer, and Maurycy, a Petersburg publisher and bookseller.

"She taught us the first things about music," wrote Julian Wieniawski, referring to his mother. "She must have been patient like an angel indeed. It was only my late brother, Henryk, who, being endowed with unusual talent and fancy for the violin, had lessons with a very gifted teacher, the late Mr. Hornziel, who some time later was hired as a soloist by the Warsaw Orchestra." When Mr. Hornziel left for Warsaw in 1841, Henryk was placed under the guidance of Mr. Stanislaw Serwaczynski, an eminent violinist, an ex-concertmaster of the Budapest Opera House, who had just returned to his native Lublin. Another name to be remembered among his teachers is that of Antoni Parys, a recognized soloist performing in Poland and Russia.

On November 18th, 1843, after a brief examination, eight-year-old Henryk Wieniawski was admitted to the Paris Conservatoire. The minimum age required of the candidates was 12, yet the professors found the boy worth the unusual concession. Henryk's mother hoped for the backing of her brother, Edward, the Conservatoire professor, yet the support was unnecessary. Henryk's talent was the sole and sufficient argument to decide in favor of the application.

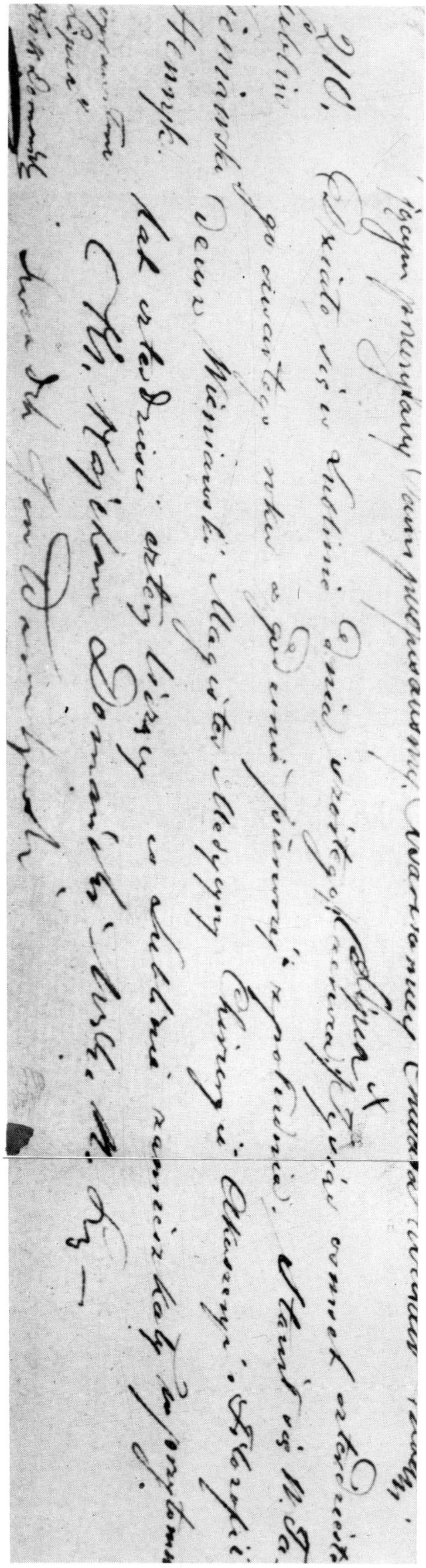

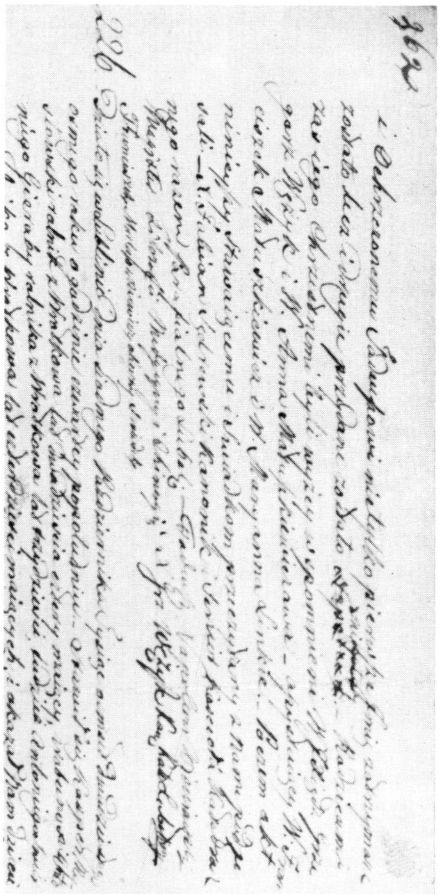

Official records of the Wieniawski family history.

Henryk's mother.　　　**Jan Hornziel.**　　　**Stanislaw Serwaczynski.**

Lublin.

The Paris Conservatoire.

A Parisian garden.

For 12 months, Henryk attended the preparatory class of professor Clavel. On December 2nd, 1844, at the request of Joseph-Lambert Massart, professor of the special class, nine-year-old Wieniawski was placed under his guidance. The professor and the student would soon strike up a lifelong friendship. After several months of studies at the Conservatoire, Henryk made his first appearance before a concert audience playing the *Symphonie concertante* of Kreutzer with his older friend, Leon Reynier, and performing Haydn's Quartet in B minor, Op. 33, as a member of the ensemble. The appearance was a considerable success, but a real triumph came only in June, 1846, when, having graduated as an all-A's-student, Wieniawski won the first prize at the final gala concert, outdistancing his much older friends including Eugène Champenois, another pride of the school, who eventually placed second. It was then that Wieniawski's mother arrived in Paris with his younger brother Jozef "who also showed musical talent."[3]

Jozef Wieniawski (1837-1912) was admitted to the piano class of the Paris Conservatoire in October, 1846. His first teachers were P.J. Zimmerman and Ch. Alkan. Having completed Zimmerman's class, he passed to A.F. Marmontel's course in 1848. Next year he was the second Wieniawski to win the first prize in his class.

After graduation, Henryk continued work with Massart until 1848, mastering violin technique. It was then that he wrote his first, still immature, compositions. "Grand Caprice Fantastique," dedicated to Massart and later published as Opus 1, was completed in 1847, when the boy was 12. Soon came another piece that he wrote in collaboration with his brother Jozef, marked "Allegro de Sonate." It was published only in 1851 and dedicated as a "tribute of friendship and acclamation" to Stanislaw Moniuszko, known as the father of Polish national opera.

Devoting a lot of time to joint exercise, the Wieniawski brothers reached the limits of the perfection that later earned them the just admiration and respect of audiences. On February 12th, 1848, they gave their first concert ever that received a very warm welcome both in the Polish emigre press (*Trzeci Maj*) and in the French (*Journal des Débats*).

Henryk attended the Paris Conservatoire as holder of a Tsar Nicolai scholarship, for which he had to play a "tribute of gratitude" in Petersburg, the imperial capital, going there for a series of recitals. The first of these, originally scheduled for April 1 (March 25 by the Julian Calendar), Wieniawski played in the Mikhailovsky Theater on April 12 (March 31) 1848, and the following one at Gentry Congregation Hall on April 27th. They both were phenomenal successes, and "let the audiences appreciate his tremendous proficiency and profound knowledge of the music." His talent was described as unique and far exceeding anything one might expect judging from the artist's age. Wiktor Karynski, the then director of the Alexandrysky Theater orchestra, devoted a lengthy and

Above and opposite: **Paris Conservatoire Records of Henryk's admission to Massart's class.**

M.ʳ **Wieniawski** 1.ᵉʳ (Henri),
né à Lublin (Pologne) le 10 juillet, 1835. (8. 2.).
(fils de Thadée Wieniawski, maître en médecine, p.ʳ chirurgie
ancien Docteur en philosophie, & de Regina Wolff). —

〜〜〜 (Violon) 〜〜〜

(admis par Décision, de l'Comité de séjour & arrêté spécial du
Ministre du 12 X.bre (**Étranger**). Classe le 6.ᵉ X.bre dans la classe
de violon de M. Clavel. — présenté par M. le Professeur Massart).
(son Prix cadet. f.ᵒ 266) — Décédé à Moscou le avril 1880

Accessit d'harmo-
nie - 1850

28 novembre.
(n.ᵒ 468).

(1.ᵉʳ Prix 1846.
(Violon).

Sorti à Russie
rayé le 1.ᵉʳ mars
1848.

revenu au Cons.ᵉ &
réadmis 6.ᵉ Div.ⁿ
le d. de M. Colin
le 11 avril 1849.

l'a servi à l'Europe
rayé le 1.ᵉʳ Fer.ⁱ
1850. —

vous sont en progrès l'assiduité auteur à ce qu'ils soient conservés.

6.ᵉ Classe préparatoire de Violon De M. Clavel. —

L'assiduité prononce unanimement la réforme De M.ʳ Roche qui n'a
pas fait de progrès et qui ne donne aucun espoir. — Il décide, en outre,
que M.M. Deloigne, Begou & Gout cessent également de
faire partie De cette classe, Dans le cas où, parmi les aspirants qui seront
examinés le 13 Décembre il se présentait des sujets qui seront
jugés plus dignes que ces derniers De savoir les reçus. —

Le jeune **Wieniawski**, polonais, est Demandé par M. Massart

Tous les élèves sont examinés, tous étaient en voie de progrès, particu-
lièrement le jeune **Wieniawski**, âgé de 10 ans 4 mois, qui donne
les plus belles espérances. —

La séance est levée à 2 heures 3/4. —

Ont signé, M.M. les Membres Du Comité.

Habeneck   Auber   Meifred

V. Batton

Postin

Wieniawski and his teacher
Massart.

Léon Reynier.

Henryk Wieniawski.

Eugène Champenois.

Concert hall of the Paris Conservatoire.

Conservatoire examination list including Henryk's brother Jozef.

Jozef at the piano.

**Henryk Wieniawski's Opus 1,
dedicated to Massart.**

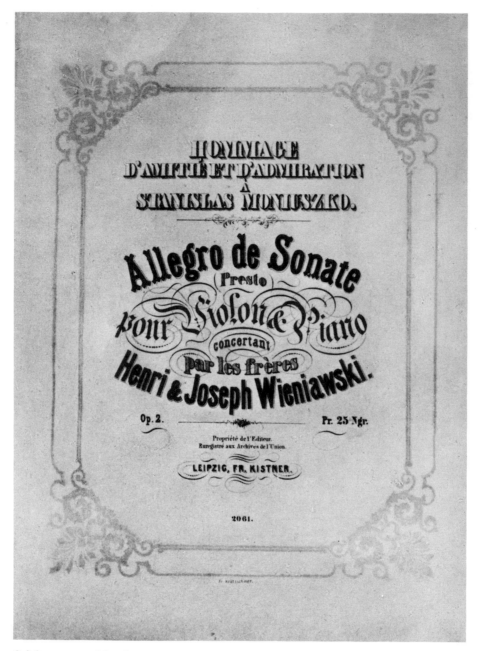

A joint composition by Henryk
and Jozef.

Revue et Gazette Musicale,
January 23, 1848.[i]

** Avant de se rendre en Russie, où l'appelle un ordre de l'empereur, le jeune Wiéniawski, violoniste de douze ans, élève de Massart, donnera, le dimanche 30 janvier, à 2 heures, une matinée musicale dans la salle de M. Sax, rue N.-St-Georges, 10. Les artistes se rappellent le succès sans exemple obtenu par le jeune virtuose au Conservatoire, où il conquit le premier prix de violon à l'unanimité, l'emportant ainsi sur des élèves presque tous doués d'un remarquable talent. Ce seul fait devrait attirer sur le jeune Wiéniawski tout l'intérêt du public; mais, de plus, ce sera pour tout le monde une grande surprise que d'écouter les compositions de cet enfant, qui peuvent rivaliser avec celles d'artistes consommés. Henri Wiéniawski exécutera le concerto qui lui a valu le premier prix au concours, et un air varié et un caprice de sa composition, avec accompagnement d'orchestre. Son jeune frère, pianiste de huit ans, élève d'Édouard Wolff, et qui donne aussi les plus grandes espérances, se fera entendre à ce concert.

Jozef and Henryk Wieniawski.

Edward Wolff.

The center of Paris.

very warm review to Wieniawski's appearances in the *Petersburg Weekly*. Another enthusiastic review by the same writer followed the farewell recital that included Henryk's own compositions.

He passed the summer at the seaside resort of Ploenen in Latvia, staying at the palace of his hospitable host and admirer of his talent Angelica de Roenne, the wife of a general. After four concerts in Petersburg, Henryk and his mother began the Baltic cities tour. The 18-year-old virtuoso amazed audiences in Helsinki, Tallin, Riga, Dorpat, and Mitava. It was decided that mother and son would arrive in Warsaw in the autumn. His elder brother Tadeusz had already begun preparations for the recitals in the capital. On the way, they made a stop in Vilnius. Wieniawski met Stanislaw Moniuszko there. The brilliant violinist would deeply respect and treasure his friendship with the eminent composer ever after. Moniuszko, in turn, despite his usual restraint in praising "children with golden hair," was enchanted by the indisputable talent of the young virtuoso. A cholera epidemic gathering its deadly harvest in Warsaw and its environs since spring that year, did not discourage multitudes from storming to the Grand Theater on the 10th of October. The tremendous success of the recital necessitated the likewise enthusiastically applauded performance of the "young maestro" on October 15.

At the end of 1848, Wieniawski left for Paris via Wroclaw and Dresden. In Wroclaw (south-western Poland) he met for the first time his "rival" Apolinary Katski, who had already won recognition among the audiences and the critics. The rivalry between the two men would continue in the years to come.

He spent more time in Dresden where the concertmaster of the Opera was Karol Lipinski. Whether Wieniawski received professional instruction from the man (as maintained by some contemporary sources)[4] is not absolutely certain. What we do know is that he played at concerts organized by Lipinski and was a frequent visitor at his home. In Leipzig, another stop on the way to the French capital, Wieniawski met Nikodem Biernacki, a violinist, composer, and the concertmaster of the local theatrical orchestra. Their relationship would remain close thereafter. In April, 1848, French journals carried this news: "Henryk Wieniawski, the young violinist, has just returned to Paris to resume his studies and successful career after a break for the triumphant tour of Russia and Poland."[5]

The brothers devoted themselves to the study of composition, Henryk under Hippolyte Collet and Jozef under Félix Le Couppey and later François Bazin. In July, 1850, both students won first prize in their classes.

The brilliant and imposing career of the Wieniawski brothers began when, having completed their composition studies, they took the road to the wide world of innumerable cities and towns, concert halls, exultant audiences, and enthusiastic reviews. Upon

St. Petersburg's Aleksandriysky Theater. *Inset:* Viktor Kazhinsky.

26

**One of Wieniawski's many
compositions for violin and piano.**

A view of St. Petersburg.

Stanislaw Moniuszko.

Facing page, *Top:* **Tallin;** *Center:*
Riga; *Bottom:* **Mitawa.**

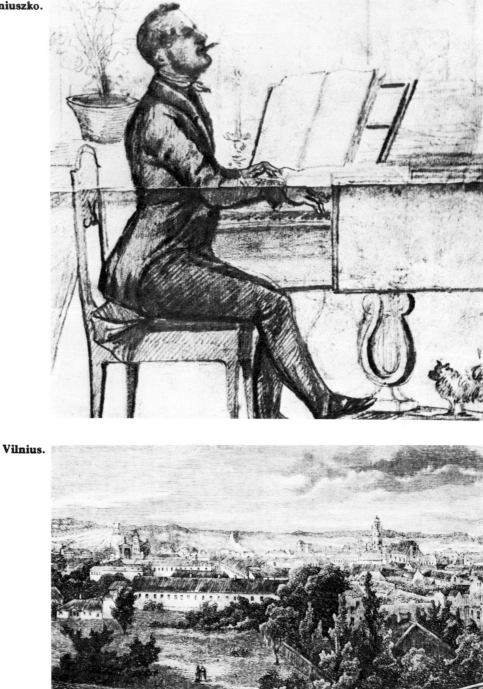

Vilnius.

Revue et Gazette Musicale, **July
30, 1848.**[ii]

manice. bret, mademoiselle Bohrer, qui a joué plusieurs fois devant la cour,
a été l'héroïne de la saison.

La liste des virtuoses étrangers qui se sont produits dans notre capitale est
déjà un peu longue ; toutefois , nous ne pouvons terminer notre lettre sans
dire quelques mots du jeune Wieniawsky, enfant de douze ans , qui a remporté
un premier prix au Conservatoire de Paris. Certes , ses progrès ont été rapides ;
il y a chez lui une maturité de talent qui a étonné ; la sûreté de son archet
se fait remarquer surtout dans le *Staccato;* mais ce qui surprend surtout à
cet âge, c'est la vivacité, la verve de son jeu ; il y a là des lueurs de génie.
Ses quatre concerts ont été très suivis. Il s'est formé sous la direction de
M. Lambert Massart. C'est l'empereur de Russie qui a fait les frais de l'éducation
musicale de Wieniawsky, jusqu'à présent le plus jeune de tous les lauréats du
Conservatoire de Paris.

Wroclaw.

Facing page: **Henryk Wieniawski.**

Karol Lipinski.

Dresden.

An excerpt for solo violin inscribed by Wieniawski to Nikodem Bernacki.

Nikodem Bernacki.

Hippolyte Collet.

Boulevard Montmartre in Paris.

List of students admitted to the composition competition of 1850.

Paris Conservatoire list of students examined in harmony.

Revue et Gazette Musicale, May 19, 1850 (continued at top of next page).[iii]

miers actes de l'*Otello* de Rossini, seront représentés par les élèves.

*** Avant de partir pour la Russie, les deux jeunes virtuoses, Henri et Joseph Wieniawski se sont fait entendre dans un concert donné par Mme Saba-

Jozef and Henryk Wieniawski.

their setting out for the first tour of Russia, *Journal des Débats* published a farewell article by Hector Berlioz, in which the composer requested of his Russian friends, the Counts Wielhorski and General Alexy Lvov, that they care for the brothers. The recital programs included their new compositions: two duets, each based respectively on the themes of Donizetti's *Lucy of Lammermoor* and the national "Tsar-and-Russia" anthem by Alexy Lvov. Henryk's own compositions were "Fantasy on *The Prophet*" by Meyerbeer and "A rustic Mazurka" dedicated to "Duchess Helena, the wife of God's servant, the late Duke Mikhail Pavlovich." In September, the brothers arrived in Warsaw. Before their appearance for the Varsovians scheduled for December, they played in the towns of Kalisz and Radom (south of Warsaw).

According to the press coverage of their concerts in Warsaw's Great Theater, the audiences were lavish of ovation and loudly aired requests for encores. The ticket money for the third recital was donated to the Unwanted Children's Center.

Challenged by an uncompromising promotion campaign conducted by the aforementioned Apolinary Katski, the brothers left for the province city of Lublin (southeast of Warsaw), where they performed until January 5, 1851. From there they went to Kiev to attend the famous "Contracts" which every year attracted the most eminent artists and audiences.

Their two concerts in Petersburg were a well-deserved success. They left upon the arrival of Apolinary Katski and embarked on a long concert tour of Russia.

Vilnius was their first stop, and the recital they gave received great acclaim. Stanislaw Moniuszko lavishly praised the brothers' musicianship:

"The restraint the reader might have observed in the assessment of the Wieniawski brothers' performances resulted from the critics' fear that one could find their possibly enthusiastic reviews exaggerated or maybe biased, a perfectly understandable feeling in view of the fact that the Polish critics had nursed the same sort of mistrust towards foreign reviews by distinguished and otherwise credible experts before they heard the Wieniawskis play. Now that there is no doubt that no other artist has ever been given such an unjust valuation (for the critics whom we used to suspect of exaggeration found Henryk to be merely one of the most talented artists), we declare that, in our view, as also in the feeling of the Polish audiences, Mr. Wieniawski ought to be classified among the most eminent maestros of violin-playing. His musicianship is a splendid blend of the widely acclaimed power of Lipinski, the tenderness of Ernst, and the humor of Paganini. And as for his technique, Vieuxtemps alone seems to be a match for him. His young brother Jozef is also a consummate musician and an excellent pianist. Chopin's music is so inaccessible that we have often seen otherwise invincible giants of the piano fall to pieces and give up. Thus, the one

Hector Berlioz.

The Marienstadt district of Warsaw.

Warsaw.

Kiev, the Pecherskaya Monastery.

Vilnius.

42

Moscow's Bolshoi Theater, with insert of a program featuring the Wieniawski brothers.

43

who shows ability to render naturally, clearly, and with true understanding such profound, mysterious, and—somehow—entangled music, undoubtedly has the right to be placed above his rivals.

"Their own duet, the frenetic march, and Henryk's marvellous mazurkas, prove how generously they are endowed with artistic genius. . ."

The tour of Russia, originally scheduled for a year, was extended by several months. They received a very warm welcome everywhere. "There was not a single large city going from Moscow to far beyond the Volga river in which the Wieniawski brothers did not perform," writes J.W. Reiss in his monograph.[6] "The obscure news about a mysterious violinist who was the alleged successor to the Paganini style and power reached the most distant places in Russia. The excited music fans awaited the arrival of the young 'magician.'. . . [7]

"The generosity and hospitality of the Russian gentry often turned a brief recital into a stay of several weeks at an estate. The brothers used the time for practicing and improvement of performance and composition. Extremely self-demanding and self-critical, rigid in judging their own work, they soon managed to develop a distinctive and very characteristic style of their own . . . the *Concert Polonaise in D-major (Polonaise brillante en ré majeur*, Op. 4) and the *Adagio élégiaque*, Op. 5 (published by Litolff in Braunschweig), the *Capriccio-Valse*, Op. 7, and *Rondo élégant,* Op. 9, no. 2 (published by Kistner in Leipzig)—all of them composed on the tour of Russia—are the most prominent examples of their masterly technique.

"*Romance sans paroles*, Op. 9, no. 1, a typically Russian romance, and *Souvenir de Moscou*, Op. 6, were intended to be the musicians' tribute to the Russian audience. Both variations woven on themes of two popular songs by Alexander Varlamov ('Krasniy sarafan' and 'Osiedlayu Konia') got the Russian audience into an ecstasy of delight."[8]

In May, 1852, the Wieniawski brothers arrived on a brief visit to Vilnius, for the spring "Contracts." As Stanislaw Moniuszko wrote in a letter to Alexander Walitsky:[9] "The Wieniawski brothers have made tremendous progress since last year; the kids have really worked very hard. However, Henryk has got it into his head to offer an overt challenge to Katski, which influences people's feelings so badly that many tend to frown upon his talent. . ."

In another letter, we find this complaint. ". . .it's nothing but worry! Katski, the Wieniawskis, Kossovski, Lada, Christiani, Mahler, Wernik. . .they all scuffle for a sweet penny and quite by chance, some of the repercussions have reached me too."[10]

Despite a very favorable assessment that the young violinist received from Moniuszko in *Kurier Wilenski*, the brothers had appearances in Vilnius before a half-empty concert hall. That prompted the decision to return to Russia for its applause.

Vladimir.

Tver.

Kremenchug.

45

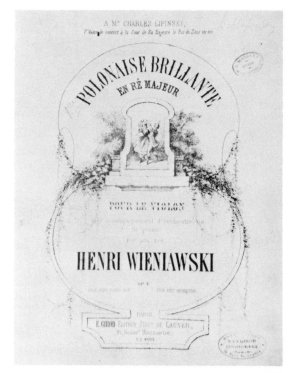

Wieniawski's opp. 4 and 5.

Wieniawski's arrangements of two
Russian folk-songs, op. 6.

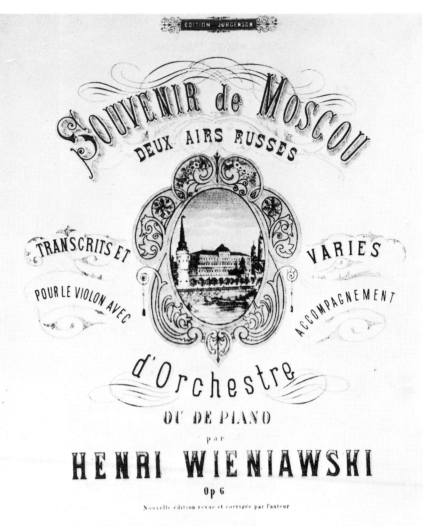

Wieniawski's op. 6 arranged for orchestra accompaniment.

A view of the Kremlin across the Moskva River.

The Wieniawski brothers.

A joint composition by Jozef and Henryk. (For Henryk, it is op. 8, for Jozef, op. 5.)

Revue et Gazette Musicale, **April 17, 1853.** [iv]

** *Vienne.* — Un ballet de M. Saint-Léon, *la Cantinière,* a été donné au théâtre de la Cour pour le bénéfice de Mme Cerrito, qui a été ravissante de verve, de gaîté et de légèreté. Mlle Marray et MM. Fraschini et Debassini ont débuté le 1er avril dans *Lucia;* c'est une des plus brillantes représentations de la saison. Mme Medori a également débuté avec beaucoup d'éclat dans *Norma.* Teresa Milanollo, que nous attendions avec la plus vive impatience, est enfin arrivée. Jusqu'ici la jeune virtuose a donné trois concerts : chaque soir la salle était comble. L'effet a été immense, les applaudissements ne discontinuaient pas, et plusieurs fois Teresa a eu les honneurs du rappel. — Les frères Wieniawski ont donné leur cinquième et dernière matinée le 8 avril. Henri a exécuté avec son talent ordinaire la première partie d'un concerto pour violon de Mendelssohn, et la fantaisie d'Ernst sur *le Pirate.* A la demande générale, il a fait entendre de nouveau *le Carnaval russe* et *les Chants russes.* La fantaisie de Thalberg sur *la Norma* a été rendue par Joseph de manière à lui mériter les applaudissements enthousiastes de toute la salle.

** *Lemberg.* — Depuis la fin du mois dernier *le Prophète* fait ch...

Having completed the well-received tour of Russia, they left for Vienna to perform in the hall of the *Gesellschaft der Musikfreunde* in March 1853.

Revue et Gazette Musicale[11] carried this report: "The Wieniawski brothers, the two young laureates of the Conservatoire whom we applauded in Paris two years ago, are a tremendous success in Vienna where they have given their third recital so far."

No matter how great the acclaim they received, it might have been even greater were it not that a famous violinist, Teresa Milanollo, the exultant critics' favorite, chose the same time for her appearances in Vienna. Wieniawski dedicated to her his *Capriccio-Valse*, Op. 7, in an eloquent gesture of enormous admiration for his prodigious rival.

After successful performances at five "music matinees," the brothers left for Leipzig and also visited several minor German towns. Arpeggio variations based on the theme of the Austrian national anthem and later included into *L'école moderne*, Op. 10, were the fruit of the Vienna episode. Cracow was lucky enough to receive the brothers, owing to a very attractive offer that Moscow had made.

The decision was made to stop touring Germany and cancel another series of recitals in Vienna.

J.W. Reiss says this about the Wieniawski Moscow performances:[12] "It all was a never-ending triumph. Henryk Wieniawski's incredibly emotional and imaginative solo-playing, his charming cantilena passages, his smashing and breathtaking virtuoso technique, and the colorfulness of his immensely refined dynamics left the audience amazed, delighted, and dazzled. The Russians were absolutely fascinated by his compositions, especially by the one dedicated to them (*Il Carnevale di Venezia*) which consisted of brilliant variations drawing on Paganini's *Venetian Carnival* and woven upon the folk song theme 'Po ulitse mostovoi.' "

From Moscow, the Wieniawski brothers travelled to Germany again. They spent a few weeks in Weimar as guests of Franz Liszt, whose critical advice proved extremely valuable for Jozef Wieniawski. They passed the summer in the Czech resorts of Karlovy Vary and Marianske Lazne, playing two recitals in each place. On their tour of the Rhineland spas, they appeared in Kissingen, Baden-Baden, Homburg, Wiesbaden, Ems, Kreuznach, and Spaa. In Baden-Baden, François-Joseph Fétis, director of the Brussels Conservatoire, invited Henryk to perform at his renowned concerts. In Spaa, the brothers were decorated with the Order of Merit. In the autumn of that year, Henryk and Jozef played in Aachen.

In October and November of 1853, they appeared at Leipzig's Gewandhaus concerts, which were attended mostly by connoisseur audiences. Even the greatest musical prodigies always considered performing at that almost legendary series a great honor. It was then that Henryk Wieniawski's Concerto in F-sharp minor, Op.

Franz Liszt.

St. Stephen's Cathedral in Vienna.

Teresa Milanollo, Henryk's great
rival.

Henryk's opp. **7 and 10**, dedicated to Teresa Milanollo and Ferdinand David, respectively.

A theater in Cracow.

Weimar.

Karlovy Vary.

Facing page, *Top:* **Entrance to Moscow's Bolshoi Theater;** *Bottom:* **Auditorium of the Bolshoi Theater.**

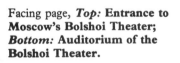

Marianske Lazne.

Cracow.

A busy Moscow street scene.

Kissingen.

Baden-Baden.

Homburg.

Wiesbaden.

Kreuznach.

Aachen.

Julius Rietz.

Facing page, *Top left:* **Henryk's op. 12;** *Top right:* **The Violin Concerto no. 1;** *Bottom:* **Leipzig.**

François-Joseph Fétis.

14, conducted by the eminent (yet, for some soloists, terrifying) Julius Rietz was first performed, receiving an enthusiastic welcome.

Their next stop was Munich, where they appeared at the Duke's court and also gave two concerts at Odeon Hall. The Duke, to whom Wieniawski dedicated his *Romance sans paroles*, Op. 9, presented them with a golden medal bearing the inscription: "En souvenir de Maximilien de Bavière."

Early in 1854, they played in Augsburg and Nürnberg.

An excerpt from news bulletin of March 1854: "Henryk and Jozef Wieniawski arrive in Berlin. Following a splendid reception at the Royal Court, where the honor of talking with their Royal Majesties was conferred upon the musicians, they rented Kroll's Theater for six concerts. The first concert took place on March 2nd."[13]

In spite of the fact that there were more musical prodigies performing in Prussia's capital then, their appearances, as Reiss says,[14] were described as "a real sensation for the Berlin concert-goers who frequently got into fights to procure themselves the tickets." They had already given over a dozen concerts, and still the fans were mobbing the ticket office.

In spring, 1854, the Wieniawski brothers paid a brief visit to Poznan. They played three excellent concerts there between the 21st and 23rd of April. They left Berlin in May. "His Majesty the King of Prussia has recently conferred the Great Golden Medal for Fine Arts on the elder of the Wieniawski brothers, enclosing also a very warm letter. Henryk and Jozef, the violinist and the pianist, are in Königsberg now. From there they are going to leave for Hanover and then to Poznan."[15] The brothers' arrival in Poznan coincided with the St. John's Eve Fair, during which, just as with the Kiev "Contracts," music lovers came to see the famous virtuosos in the Music Fair Hall. The Poznan correspondent of *Revue et Gazette Musicale* reported that the "Wieniawski duo have already given twelve recitals, a figure which conveys how tremendous a popularity they enjoy here. The Polish duet which the young artists played four times as an encore was a remarkable success."[16]

Also greatly acclaimed were Henryk's mazurkas, including *Souvenir de Posen*, written for and dedicated to Poznan music lovers.

They spent August in the spas of the Rhineland, and, after a brief rest, embarked on a new long tour of Munich, Ostend, and Würzburg.

Then, another concert series in Frankfurt-on-the-Main at the invitation of Fétis. In their first appearance in Brussels, both brothers attained incredible success and rose to an eminence which endured long after. In Hamburg, the enthusiastic audience encored them at least twelve times.

Then Paris again. Massart held a gala reception in honor of his

The first page of Henryk Wieniawski's op. 9, dedicated to Maximilian of Bavaria.

ROMANCE SANS PAROLES ET RONDO ÉLÉGANT

Henri WIENIAWSKI op: 9

à son Altesse Monseigneur
le Duc MAXIMILIEN de BAVIÈRE.

Facing page, *Top:* **Munich;** *Bottom:* **Augsburg.**

Revue et Gazette Musicale, December 25, 1853.[v]

. *Munich.* — Le concert donné par les frères Wieniawski dans la salle de l'Odéon, a été un véritable événement. L'enthousiasme du nombreux public allait toujours croissant ; les deux virtuoses ont été fréquemment interrompus par les plus chauds applaudissements, et ont eu plusieurs fois les honneurs du rappel. On annonce que la grande salle du Théâtre-Royal, nouvellement restaurée, sera inaugurée le lundi de Noël. — Le théâtre de la Cour, qui a été complétement restauré, sera inauguré par les *Croisés,* opéra de Bénédict.

. *Francfort.* — Teresa Milanollo a donné, le 17 décembre, son premier

Revue et Gazette Musicale, March 19, 1854.[vi]

. Les frères Wieniawski ont donné leur second concert à Berlin le 9 de ce mois. L'auditoire ne comptait pas moins de 1,600 personnes, et les deux jeunes virtuoses ont été rappelés quinze fois dans le cours de la séance.

Revue et Gazette Musicale, March 26, 1854.[vii]

le prodigieux talent du célèbre violoniste, qui a reçu ici, comme partout, un accueil enthousiaste. Vieuxtemps se propose de donner une série de concerts, et le public ne lui fera pas défaut, malgré la gravité des conjonctures politiques. Le troisième a dû avoir lieu le 20 du courant. — Les frères Wieniawski en sont à leur quatrième soirée, qui probablement ne sera pas la dernière. — Mme Jenny Lind a fait ses adieux au public ; d'ici, la célèbre vittuose se rend à Vienne.

Nürnberg.

Berlin.

The Kroll Theater in Berlin.

From left to right: **Clara Wieck-Schumann; Jenny Lind; Teresa Milanollo.**

From left to right: **Julius Schulhof; Antonio Bazzini; Heinrich Wilhelm Ernst.**

A view of Poznan.

Dziś w Niedzielę dnia 23. Kwietnia 1854.

ABONAMENT ZNIESIONY.

OSTATNI KONCERT
Braci Wieniawskich.

Przed tém

Wesoły, czyli: Chórysta w podróży.

Komedya ze śpiewami w dwóch aktach przez L. Schneider. Muzyka przez rozmaitych kompozytorów.

OSOBY:

Dziedzic Degen, rotmistrz wysłużony	Pan Rennert.
Thusnelda, jego córka	Panna Krebs.
Hermaphrosena, jego krewna	Pani Rennert.
Anna	Panna Göthe.
Wesoły, chórysta z Berlina	Pan Reusche.
Walter, referendaryusz	Pan Schöneich.
Fabian, stary sługa	Pan Fischer.

Poczém nastąpi:

Wielki Koncert Braci Wieniawskich.

PROGRAM.

1) Uwertura z „Oberona" przez C. M. Webera.
2) Air varié przez Vieuxtemps, wykonane przez **Henryka Wieniawskiego**.
3) Ricci – Walec, śpiewany przez panią **Flintzer-Haupt**.
4) Capriccio brillanto na fortepian z towarzyszeniem orkiestry przez Mendelsohna, wykonane przez Józefa **Wieniawskiego**.
5) Adagio elique i Polonaise à la guaidiera, skomponowane i wykonane przez pana **Henryka Wieniawskiego**.
6) Wielka aria z Oberona: „Oceanie potworo", przez C. M. Webera, śpiewana przez panią **Flintzer-Haupt**.
7) Barkerole na fortepian, kompozycya i wykonanie pana Józefa **Wieniawskiego**.
8) Souvenir de Moscou, kompozycya i wykonanie pana **Henryka Wieniawskiego**.

Pani **Flintzer-Haupt** przyobiecała współdziałanie przez łaskawą grzeczność dla **Dyrekcyi.**

Otwarcie kassy o godzinie 6. Początek o godzinie 7.

Ceny miejsc przy kassie we dnie i wieczorem:

Loża obcych 1 Tal. Loża pierwszego piętra, drugi Balkon i Krzesło 20 Sgr. Parter 12½ Sgr. Loża drugiego piętra 10 Sgr. Amfiteatr 6 Sgr. Galerya 4 Sgr. Bilety na Parter dla dzieci 7½ Sgr.
Biletów dostać można od godziny 9. do 1. i od 3. do 5. przy kassie teatralnéj.

Jutro niebędzie przedstawienia.

We Wtorek pierwsze przedstawienie gościnne panny **T. Sołdańskiéj** i pana **Ehrich**, solotancerzy przy Król. nadwornym teatrze w Berlinie. Do tego, po raz pierwszy: **Stary Muzykant**, komedya przez autora „Sieroty z Lowood".

Fr. Wallner.

Poznań, nakładem W. Deckera i Spółki.

A bill in Polish for the April 23, 1854 concert in Poznan of the Wieniawski brothers.

Stadttheater in Posen.

Heute Sonntag den 23. April 1854.

ABONNEMENT SUSPENDU.

Letztes Concert

der

Gebr. Wieniawski.

Vor demselben:

Fröhlich, oder: Der Chorist auf Reisen.

Komisches Liederspiel in zwei Akten von L. Schneider. Musik von verschiedenen Meistern.

Personen

Gutsbesitzer von Degen, Rittmeister a. D.	Herr Rennert.
Thusnelde, seine Tochter	Fräulein Krebs.
Hermaphrosine von Quengel, seine Cousine	Frau Rennert.
Anna	Fräulein Gothe.
Fröhlich, Chorist aus Berlin	Herr Reusche.
Referendarius von Walter	Herr Schoneich.
Fabian, ein alter Diener des Rittmeisters	Herr Fischer.

Hierauf:

Großes Concert der Gebrüder Wieniawski.

PROGRAMM.

1. Ouverture aus „Oberon" von C. M. v. Weber.
2. Air varié von Vieuxtemps, vorgetragen von Heinrich Wieniawski.
3. Ricci-Walzer, gesungen von Frau Flinzer-Haupt.
4. Capricio brillante für Clavier mit Orchesterbegleitung von Mendelssohn, vorgetragen von Joseph Wieniawski.
5. Adagio elique und Polonaise à la gualdiera, componirt und vorgetragen von Heinrich Wieniawski.
6. Große Arie aus Oberon: „Ozean du Ungeheuer" von C. M. v. Weber, vorgetragen von Frau Flinzer-Haupt.
7. Barkerole für Clavier, componirt und vorgetragen von Joseph Wieniawski.
8. Souvenir de Moscou, componirt und vorgetragen von Heinrich Wieniawski.

Frau Flinzer-Haupt hat aus Gefälligkeit für die Direktion ihre Mitwirkung freundlichst zugesagt.

Preise der Plätze für Tages- und Abendkasse:

Fremdenloge 1 Rthlr. Erster Rang, Zweiter Ballon und Sperrsitz 20 Sgr. Parterre 12½ Sgr. Zweiter Rang 10 Sgr. Amphitheater 6 Sgr. Gallerie 4 Sgr. Kinderbillets in's Parterre 7½ Sgr. Billets sind von 9 bis 1 Uhr und von 3 bis 5 Uhr im Theatergebäude an der Kasse zu haben.

Geübte Schreiber finden Beschäftigung.

Morgen bleibt die Bühne geschlossen.

Dienstag: Erstes Gastspiel der Fräulein P. Soldanski und des Herrn Erich, Solotänzer des Königl. Hoftheaters in Berlin. — Dazu zum Erstenmale: Ein alter Musikant, Schauspiel von der Verfasserin des Drama's: „Die Waise aus Lowood."

Fr. Wallner.

Posen, gedruckt bei B. Decker & Comp.

A bill in German for the April 23 concert.

68

The Wieniawski duo. (Henryk is
seated.)

Henryk's "Memory of Poznan."

Revue et Gazette Musicale,
August 13, 1854.[viii]

Revue et Gazette Musicale,
September 19, 1854.[ix]

Revue et Gazette Musicale,
October 1, 1854.[x]

Fair in Munich.

Ostend.

A collection of some of the great virtuosos of the middle of the nineteenth century. From left to right (standing): **Eckert, Sainton, Vieuxtemps, Deloffe, Hill, Laub, Sivori, Bottesini, Pauer, Piatti, Pillet, Menter(?), Seligmann, Bennett, Ella, Bougniet;** From left to right (seated): **Ernst, Hallé.**

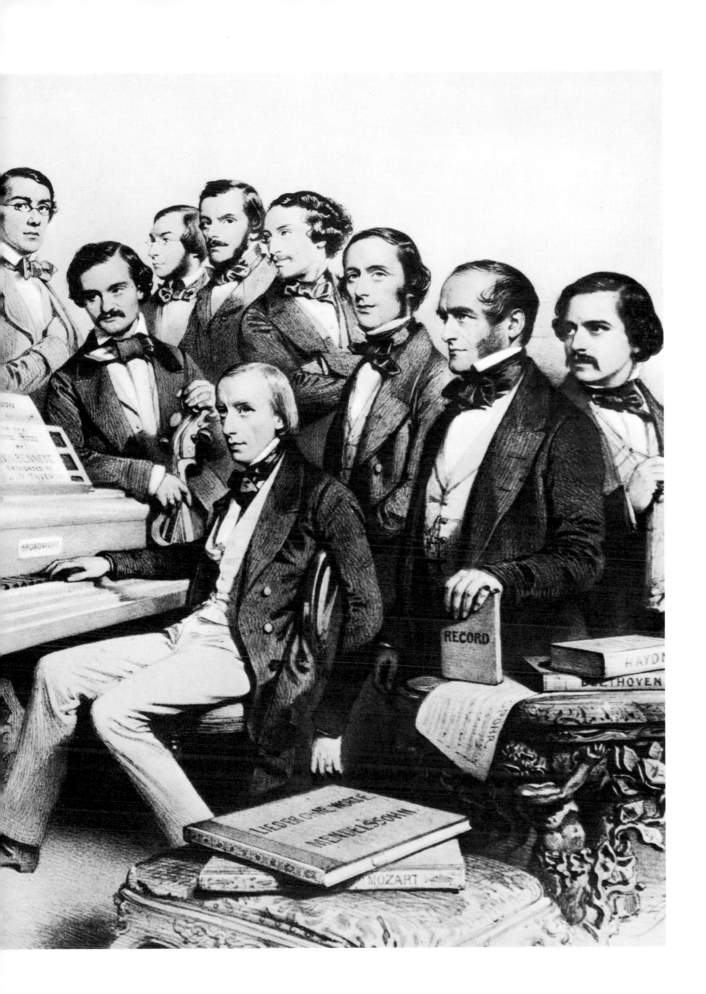

Paris.

Joseph-Lambert Massart.

Brussels.

Würzburg.

former student. It was then that Henryk and Hector Berlioz, who once praised Wieniawski's talent in *Journal des Débats*, had a spirited argument that highlighted a difference of opinion between the artist and the critic.

In the spring of 1855, the brothers returned with their mother to their home-town of Lublin. Reiss writes,[17] "Their last joint appearance was in Kiev, and several months later Henryk began another tour alone. The brothers, who had always been one, parted! The reason why remained unknown. The fact is that their career split them. . ." Reiss himself solves the riddle in another part of his monograph when he refers to the German critic Ludwig Rellstab's opinion (shared by some other experts) that performing together cramped both musicians and denied them their individuality. They simply eclipsed each other.[18]

In August of that year, Henryk went for medical treatment to the spa of Szczawno (Salzbrunn).[19] His treatment did not prevent him from entertaining the visitors in the local "Kursaal," where he appeared several times in August and September.

In October, he appeared again at the inaugural concert in the Gewandhaus, long after the split with Jozef. The conductors were Julius Rietz and Henryk's close friend Ferdinand David, the first concertmaster of the Leipzig theatrical orchestra. A year before, Henryk had dedicated to the latter his *L'École moderne*, Op. 10. Another piece, *Thème original varié*, was dedicated to Raimund Dreyschock, a recognized violinist, professor of the Leipzig conservatory and concertmaster of the Gewandhaus orchestra.

In November and December, Wieniawski turned a series of recitals in Cologne into a phenomenal success.

Early in 1856, he arrived in Antwerp, then made his way to Brussels, and in mid-March he left for Holland.

"The tour of Holland lasted much longer than Wieniawski had originally expected. He gave 45 recitals within a single season. The itinerary included Utrecht, Amsterdam (where he played three times in a single week), Rotterdam, Leyden, and The Hague. Astounded and dazzled audiences would long remember his solo playing and the performance of Beethoven violin sonatas with Auguste Dupont, one of the most eminent pianists of the Belgian school. Medals and distinctions were showered on him again. After the first concert, the delighted audience serenaded him by the light Chinese lanterns. His lithographed portrait was being sold as well as drawings and copper engravings. The sculptor Lacomblé made his bust, which was displayed in The Hague's Royal Gallery. Henryk was made an honorary member of the music society 'Toekomst' and of the 'Diligentia' orchestra. Invited to the court of the Dutch King William, a great music lover, Wieniawski played at the summer residence in Loo and was granted the title of Knight of the Oak Tree Crown Order. In the address after the farewell concert, the chairman of the Theatrical Committee paid tribute to Wieniawski's artistic genius.

Ferdinand David.

Facing page, *Top:* **Szczawno;** *Bottom:* **The concert hall of the Gewandhaus in Leipzig.**

Raimund Dreyschock.

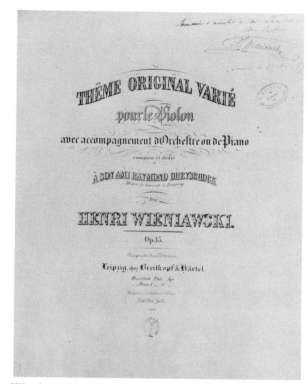

Wieniawski's op. 15.

Antwerp.

.·. *Leipzig.* — *L'Etoile du Nord* a été représentée pour la première fois, le 4 octobre, au théâtre de la ville, avec une mise en scène et une exécution dignes du chef-d'œuvre. Nous n'avons pas besoin d'ajouter que le succès a été complet. Le premier concert du Gewandhaus a eu lieu sous la direction de MM. Rietz et David. On y a entendu, entre autres, Mme de Holdorp, cantatrice, et H. Wieniawski, le célèbre violoniste, qui a été salué de bruyants applaudissements à plusieurs reprises, et surtout après la fameuse fantaisie de Paganini.

Revue et Gazette Musicale,
October 21, 1855. [xi]

.·. Henri Wieniawski, le célèbre violoniste, est maintenant à Berlin. Dans son voyage en Pologne, il a donné à Lublin, sa ville natale, un concert dont le produit était destiné à la fondation d'une salle d'asile pour les jeunes orphelins. Le concert a produit 5,000 florins, et le virtuose y a obtenu un succès immense, en jouant plusieurs de ses compositions : une grande fantaisie sur *la Sonnambula*, une polka de concert et *Souvenirs de Lublin*, romance variée, dédiée aux dames de cette ville.

.·. M. Théodore de Witt, musicien distingué, qui s'est fait avantageu-

Revue et Gazette Musicale,
January 6, 1856. [xii]

Revue et Gazette Musicale,
January 13, 1856. [xiii]

.·. C'est, non pas Henri Wieniawski, le violoniste, mais son frère Joseph, le pianiste, qui a donné à Lublin, sa ville natale, le concert dont nous avons parlé dans notre dernier numéro. Henri Wieniawski est encore en ce moment à Bruxelles.

Cologne.

Henryk Wieniawski.

Utrecht.

80

A caricature of Lassen and Wieniawski (*Eulenspiegel*, July 13, 1856).

"However, perhaps the most valuable treasure Wieniawski found in Holland was the friendship he struck up with Alexandre Desfossez, an admirer of his talent and author of the first and only study on Wieniawski at that time."[20]

The triumphant tour of Holland lasted almost a year with a brief intermission in the summer for the customary visit to the Rhineland. As a result, he had to postpone his appearances in London and Paris.

In 1857 the audiences in Poland saw the brothers on stage together again. In April and May they played eight concerts in Lvov, each of which was a bigger success than the one before.

Cracow was the next stop on the route. Their first concert on May 15 was a financial fiasco. The paper *Czas* carried this comment:[21] "The only conceivable reason why, was that the world famous circus troupe chose the same time for its performance." Yet, at the following two concerts, there was standing room only, and the ovation was incredible. Having left Cracow, Henryk, without his brother, made his way to Königsberg and then to Poznan to the great convention of artists held annually on the occasion of the St. John's Eve Fair. In July, back for health-resort treatment to Salzbrunn.

In the late summer, Wieniawski continued his well-deserved recreation in the seaside resorts of southern France. Nevertheless, he found time to appear on stage in Marseille and Bordeaux. In September, he was back at work for good in the Rhineland.

The Baden-Baden palace of Grand Duchess Helen, like her Petersburg residence, was a Mecca for the greatest musical prodigies. Even facing the competition of such excellent violinists as Panofka, Ernst, Sivori, and Sighicelli, Wieniawski always remained unrivalled. "Mrs. Muchanov-Kalergis, who happened to be in Baden-Baden, said this in a letter to her daughter: 'The Grand Duchess Helen is going to be here for another four weeks. She has promised to invite some musical celebrities here including Anton Rubinstein and heavenly Wieniawski.' In another letter, she described him thus: 'Wieniawski is the world's most prominent virtuoso; he has a Lisztian talent and glorious prospects at his 22 years of age. We three played a Schumann quintet and finally the famous Beethoven variations in his [Wieniawski's] new, wonderful arrangement.' "[22]

In March, 1858, after a glorious tour of Germany, Belgium, and Holland where he played with Messrs. Fiorentini and Giovanni Bottesini, Henryk Wieniawski arrived in Paris. In April and May he made several magnificent appearances including one with Anton Rubinstein, thenceforth his best friend.

From France back to Belgium, where he had always received an enthusiastic welcome. In the summer, the name of Wieniawski could be found among the stars of the Wiesbaden festival. In October, he gave a very successful concert in Dresden, and, late in

Aleksander Zarzycki, a virtuoso pianist who also performed in Poznan.

Hans von Bülow.

The first biography of Wieniawski.

Revue et Gazette Musicale,
December 7, 1856.[XV]

.*. *Wiesbade.* — La saison des concerts touche à sa fin. Dans ces derniers temps, nous n'avons rien d'important à signaler, si ce n'est la deuxième soirée de M. Arthur Napoléon. Henri Wieniawski se trouve ici en ce moment; mais nous ignorons si nous aurons le plaisir de l'entendre. Le théâtre de la ville a mis à l'étude *Casilda,* opéra du duc de Saxe-Cobourg.

Revue et Gazette Musicale,
October 26, 1856.[XIV]

.*. *La Haye.* — Mme Stoltz poursuit le cours de ses brillantes représentations. *L'Etoile du Nord* est en pleine répétition. Henri Wieniawski, qui a été ici, comme partout ailleurs, le héros de nos concerts de l'an dernier, est de nouveau en Hollande pour toute la saison. On lui prépare de grandes ovations. La cantatrice de la Haye toujours tant applaudie, Mme Offermans van Hove, a obtenu, comme le célèbre violoniste, le plus grand succès.

Henryk Wieniawski.

The Hague.

Jozef and Henryk.

Lwow.

A view of Cracow.

86

Market-place in Poznan.

Marseille.

Bordeaux.

St. Petersburg.

Baden-Baden.

Henry Litolff.

Henri Herz.

Anton Rubinstein.

Giacomo Meyerbeer.

Heinrich Wilhelm Ernst.

Camillo Sivori.

Maria Muchanov-Kalergis.

Grand Duchess Helen Pavlovna.

Henryk Wieniawski.

1858, arrived in London at long last. A London musical columnist carried this report: "Wieniawski's first appearance in the Lyceum Theatre was both splendid and very noisy . . . the uproar that never stopped throughout the concert, finally erupted as thunderous ovation for the violinist whom Jullien hired for his first-ever two-month-long tour of England. The Lyceum recital was one of the most convincing victories we have ever seen."[23]

At that time, chamber music enjoyed enormous popularity among London music lovers. According to Reiss: "To nurture string quartets, the Beethoven Quartet Society was formed, invitations to whose musical activities were considered a great honor. Regular concerts of chamber music, initiated by John Ella (violinist of the Philharmonic Society), were held in London since 1845. His successor was Thomas Chappell—the founder of Monday Popular-Concerts, whose real *spiritus movens* was his brother, Arthur. The rule of featuring only an outstanding player at every concert, consistency in programming, timing of appearances, and, finally, superb quality performance by the most prominent artists, were the factors underlying the success of the undertaking. It is no wonder that the concerts soon assumed the proportions of a major musical event in London. Wieniawski was invited to play first violin in a quartet and quintet by Mendelssohn at the inauguration of the Monday Popular Concerts on February 14th, 1859. He appeared then with Louis Ries, Doyle, Schreuss, and Piatti. At the following concerts, featuring Haydn, Mozart, and Beethoven quartets, Wieniawski was replaced as first violinist by H.G. Blagrove and Prosper Sainton, an excellent soloist and composer of brilliant violin music. Wieniawski also performed for the Beethoven Quartet Society, playing the viola with the irresistible vigor which had already become his cachet. The other members of the quartet were Ernst on first violin, Joachim on second, and Piatti on cello, an unrivalled ensemble in its own time and for many years to come. It must really have been a wonderful sound and the mood must have been overwhelming too, especially in adagio, when every superb ensemble-member could sing out a heavenly cantilena on magnificent old Italian instruments."[24]

Reiss mentions the following characteristics of Wieniawski off-stage:[25] "He had all the virtues of high society: elegant manners and the talent to move people's hearts. His personal charm was simply irresistible. He felt at home everywhere. An unequalled *causeur*, he could always keep those in his company enchanted. Said a Vienna daily columnist, 'In my opinion Wieniawski might well be equally popular should he choose to speak to his audience about the Polonaise in A major, instead of playing it. By all means he would make a good orator, for he is a most charming and most brilliant *causeur*, particularly on his good days and when not afflicted by his rheumatic pains. On such occasions, his wit is indomitable and exuberant. Wieniawski is a virtuoso of conversation indeed.' "

**A letter from Wieniawski to an
unknown addressee.**[XVI]

CHRONIQUE ÉTRANGÈRE.

.*. *Londres.* — Les concerts de Jullien sont très-suivis. Deux soirées intitulées : *Mendelssohn's Night* et *Beethoven's Night*, dans lesquelles on n'a exécuté que des œuvres de ces deux grands maîtres, ont surtout attiré beaucoup de monde. La célèbre pianiste, miss Arabella Goddard, et Henri Wieniawski s'y sont fait entendre : ils ont été très-favorablement accueillis. — On parle de la construction d'un nouveau palais de Cristal au nord de Londres, et dans lequel se trouveraient plusieurs grandes salles de concert. Les frais sont évalués à 1,250,000 fr.

**Revue et Gazette Musicale,
November 28, 1858.**[XVII]

**Revue et Gazette Musicale,
February 27, 1859.**[XVIII]

.*. Henri Wieniawski n'obtient pas moins de succès à Londres, en exécutant la musique de Mendelssohn, qu'en jouant ses propres compositions. C'est ce qui vient de lui arriver tout récemment dans un concert, où il a interprété un quintetto du maître de manière à obtenir les honneurs du rappel.

London traffic.

Henryk Wieniawski.

A bill for the rehearsal of the London quartet.

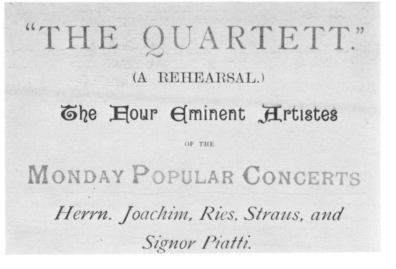

For all the popularity he enjoyed in England, Wieniawski avoided high society. He felt offended by the elite's attitude towards the profession of artist—a blend of enormous expectation and lack of respect. Nevertheless, he yielded to Rubinstein's persuasion and paid a visit to the Hampton family, most probably because Mrs. Hampton, a great music lover herself, was the sister of George Osborne, the well-known pianist and composer.

The daughter of the house, Isabel, would soon become Wieniawski's wife. Mrs. Hampton-Wieniawski wrote in her diary that her mother who had already heard him onstage was extremely happy about the prospect of his first visit and expected him impatiently. He arrived in April, 1859. She explains that she does not mean to make her story a novel, and so will not go into detail, merely saying that she and the famous artist soon felt sentiments of love for each other and soon became engaged.[26]

As usual, Wieniawski spent the summer season of 1859 in the Rhineland spas of Ems and Homburg and in a visit to Ostend, where he called on Isabel and her mother.

It was then that, by all accounts, Wieniawski wrote his famous romantic *Legend*. However, one may seriously doubt the rumor that the composition was performed before he got Isabel's father's blessing for the couple, as maintained in the *Tygodnik Ilustrowany.*[27] Sir Brian Dean Paul, Henryk's grandson, says that Thomas Hampton disinherited his daughter for the marriage.

In the autumn of 1859, Wieniawski played at a number of symphonic and chamber concerts in London. Among other things, he appeared in the Schiller Festival at the famous Crystal Palace.

In April of 1860, Wieniawski left for Petersburg to accept officially the appointment he received in August of 1859 as "His Majesty's soloist and soloist of the imperial theaters."

A music correspondent submitted this news: "Henryk Wieniawski received a very warm welcome as he performed at the Grand Theater. The enthusiasm was rapidly building, and, by the end of the night, the delighted audience burst into an ecstatic ovation. The violinist played a Mendelssohn concerto and *Venetian Carnival* and three or four charming and very novel compositions, which hint that his future success as a composer may well be as great as the glory he has already found as a virtuoso. The audience was shouting requests for his own compositions, so that he had to give three encores. As for *Venetian Carnival*, Wieniawski lent it a quality of novelty. . ."[28]

In June, Wieniawski played in Warsaw and in Vilnius. In July, he went to Paris for his wedding.

On August 8, 1860, he pledged marriage vows to Isabel Bessie-Hampton at St. Andrew's in Paris. The couple hurried back to Poland to see Henryk's parents at his home-town of Lublin.

Recalling her first moments as the artist's wife, Isabel mentioned all-night coach-travel from Warsaw, for there was no railway con-

A quartet rehearsal.

Homburg. Skrzypek *Wieniawski Henryk* koncertował tu z wielkiem powodzeniem-—Nabył on od Bériota ulubione jego skrzypce roboty Maginiego, za 24,000 franków. W Ostendzie grał z *Piattim* basetlistą, oraz fortepianistą *Rubinstejnem*; (przyjmowani byli z zapałem). Mówią o nim, że ma zaślubić siostrzenicę kompozytora Osborne.

Ruch Muzyczny, October 5, 1859.[xix]

Charles de Bériot.

.*. *Ostende.* — Notre saison de bains a été cette année des plus brillantes, non-seulement par la présence des plus hauts personnages, parmi lesquels se trouvaient S. M. le roi des Belges, S. A. I. la grande-duchesse Hélène, le prince régent de Prusse, le duc de Brabant, le comte de Flandres, etc., etc., mais aussi par la réunion d'un grand nombre de célébrités musicales: Rubinstein, Piatti, Wieniawski, Haumann, M. et Mme de Blaes, le comte de Stainlein, M. et Mme Léonard, Edouard Wolff, le violoncelliste Poorten, le violoniste russe Bezekirski, le ténor Wicart, telle était la pléiade d'artistes appelés à se faire entendre devant nos augustes hôtes. Inutile d'ajouter qu'ils se sont acquittés de cette tâche avec la supériorité qui les distingue. Le succès du premier concert donné au Casino a été si complet qu'on s'occupe d'organiser une seconde fête musicale du même genre, et M. Léonard a été tellement émerveillé du jeu de M. Wieniawski qu'il lui a proposé de faire un quatuor dans lequel nous entendrons, avec Wieniawski et Léonard, Bezekirski et Piatti. Malheureusement Wieniawski est malade et garde le lit. Il est fiancé à une jeune Anglaise. En partant, la grande-duchesse Hélène lui a laissé une magnifique broche avec des pendants d'oreille en diamants pour sa fiancée.

Revue et Gazette Musicale, November 11, 1859.[xx]

Ems. Król Hollenderski przytomny na koncercie basetlisty *Piattego* i skrzypka *Wieniawskiego*, obdarował tamtego orderem „dębowym," a tego pierścieniem mającym cyfrę królewską z dyamentów ułożoną.

Ruch Muzyczny, October 12, 1859.[xxi]

— P. Henryk *Wieniawski* (skrzypek) ma się udać wkrótce do Petersburga na stałe mieszkanie w charakterze pierwszego skrzypka dworu J. C. K. Mości.

Ruch Muzyczny, August 31, 1859.[xxii]

— Henryk *Wieniawski* nie nabył jeszcze skrzypiec roboty Magginiego, za które właściciel ich Bériot żąda 20,000 franków. Odłożono stanowczy co do tego kupna układ, do bytności obu artystów w Petersburgu, gdzie się téj zimy obaj spotkać mają, i gdzie pierwsi tegocześni skrzypkowie zjechać się zamierzają. Będzie tam bowiem także Vieuxtemps i Laub.

Ruch Muzyczny, November 9, 1859.[xxiii]

Ems.

Wieniawski's famous "Légende,"
dedicated to his English bride.

English aristocrats on horses.

London's Crystal Palace.

.*. *Londres.* — La troupe italienne de Drury-Lane vient de donner la *Marta* de M. de Flotow, avec Mlle Titiens dans le rôle principal, et Giuglini dans celui de Lyonel. — La *Dinorah* anglaise de Coventgarden en est à sa cinquantième représentation. — Le festival Schiller a été célébré au palais de Cristal de la manière la plus brillante : musique, banquet, discours, marche aux flambeaux, rien n'y a manqué. Le temps était magnifique, et quinze mille personnes, tant Allemands qu'Anglais, y assistaient. La presse anglaise s'est distinguée en honorant la mémoire du grand poëte de l'Allemagne, et ses représentants étaient nombreux au palais de Cristal. La fête a commencé par un discours plein de verve et d'inspiration prononcé par M. Kuckel. Le morceau principal du concert était la cantate due à la plume habile et élevée de M. Freiligrath, mise en musique par M. Pauer, avec tout le talent qui dénote un musicien consommé. Le solo de Wicniawski (l'unique solo du concert) a été couvert de bravos. Vers cinq heures une procession aux flambeaux portés par huit cents jeunes gens des deux nations allemande et anglaise, dans les jardins du palais, et suivie d'un banquet, a dignement terminé cette belle journée.

Revue et Gazette Musicale,
November 20, 1859.[XXIV]

Revue et Gazette Musicale,
November 27, 1859.[XXV]

.*. *Londres.* — Les *Popular Concerts* de Saint-James hall sont très-suivis cette année. A la dernière séance on a surtout remarqué MM. Ch. Hallé, Wieniawski, Piatti et Mme Lemmens-Scherrington. Cette dernière a remporté un succès hors ligne en chantant de la façon la plus distinguée le *Chant de mai*, l'une des plus suaves mélodies de Meyerbeer.

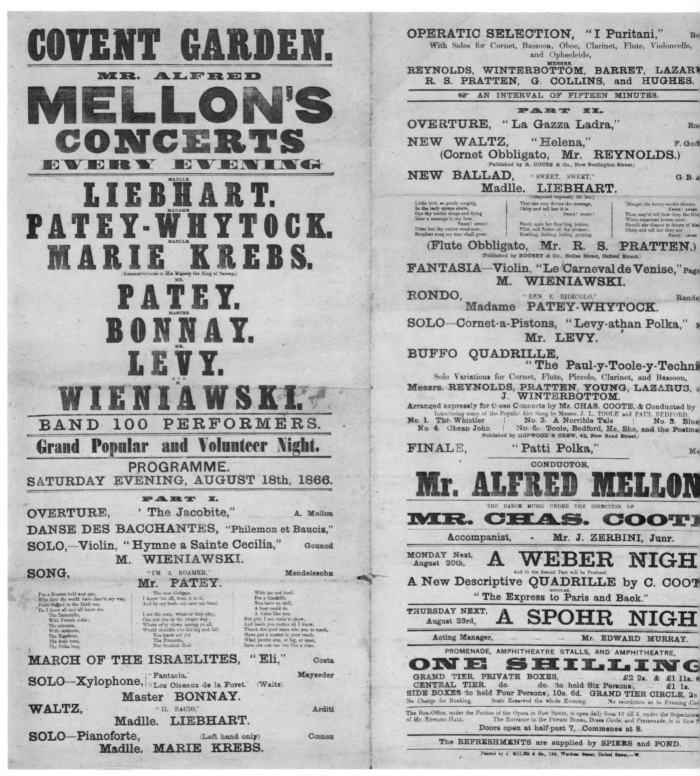

Programs for two of Wieniawski's London concerts of 1866 and 1858 (courtesy of Dr. Herbert R. Axelrod).

105

The first and last pages of the manuscript of Wieniawski's "Légende."

8.
Sul A
espressivo
Violoncello
espressivo
Poco animato
ritenuto
Flauti

A concert in the Crystal Palace.

The interior of St. Petersburg's Grand Theater.

A Warsaw fountain.

Isabel Bessie-Hampton,
Wieniawski's bride.

Wieniawski's home-town of Lublin, where he brought his new wife to meet his parents.

nection. They arrived in Lublin around 7 a.m. The people, the language, the clothes were so new and odd to her that she did not even notice the journey was over. Her parents-in-law gave them the traditional Polish bread-and-salt welcome, which items were on a silver plate. She described her stay at the Wieniawskis' house as charming and happy days. They were guests at numerous receptions and "at a ball at the governor's" where for the first time she saw the mazurka danced.[29] When the honeymoon was over, Mr. and Mrs. Wieniawski travelled to Petersburg via Warsaw. Now that Henryk had got the appointment, they would settle in Russia's capital for good. Isabel mentions a very warm welcome Henryk's friends gave them upon their arrival in Warsaw. They showed respect and admiration for Henryk and most cordial kindness to his wife. "Warsaw was wonderful," she says in her memoirs. She was deeply moved by the Polish hospitality she experienced. In Warsaw she was introduced to her husband's eminent friends Stanislaw Moniuszko and Mr. Muchanov-Kalergis. At the house of Mrs. Muchanov, they met Helena Modrzejewska, the almost legendary actress. Isabel had already seen her in *Romeo and Juliet* and admired her talent very much, even though, not knowing the Polish language, she could only appreciate the visual aspects of her acting and the sound of her voice. The actress told her she had always dreamt of learning English well enough to do Shakespeare plays in the original language.

Giulia Grisi.

Facing the prospect of tiring travel by train with numerous changes and inconveniences, Wieniawski hired a horse-drawn coach, and they set off for the town of Gatczyna, from where they took a train to Petersburg. It did not take them a very long time to find a neat and well-furnished flat on Bolshaya Morskaya Street.[30]

Warsaw's Saski Gardens.

According to Reiss: "The Russian Musical Society set up in 1859 was the heart of Petersburg musical life, with Anton Rubinstein (its founder) and Matthew Wielhorski as directors, and Grand Duchess Helena Pavlovna as the patron. Wieniawski was a soloist at the Society's symphonic concerts.

Adelina Patti.

". . .Petersburg audiences were lucky enough to hear and watch the greatest vocal prodigies on the stage of the Opera House. To mention but the most widely acclaimed guest performances, there were the tenors Giuseppe Mario and his equally famous wife Giulia Grisi, Enrico Tamberlick, the coloratura Adelina Patti, the dramatic soprano Christina Nilsson, as also Graziani and Nantier-Didiée, who received tributes of admiration at major European opera houses. Those artists were also close friends and frequent visitors at the home of the Wieniawski family."[31]

Wieniawski spent twelve years in Petersburg as "soloist of His Majesty the Tsar." He earned great authority among the ruling family, a reputation as the aristocrats' favorite, to say nothing of his tremendous popularity among ordinary concert-goers. The Tsar's brother, Grand Prince Konstanty, was a passionate lover of chamber music.

Anton Rubinstein.

Matthew Wielhorski.

Christina Nilsson.

Constance Nantier-Didiée.

Giuseppe Mario.

Enrico Tamberlick.

Teodor Leszetycki, piano teacher at the new St. Petersburg Conservatory.

Aleksander Dreyschock, another piano teacher at the Conservatory.

His court, and in particular his summer residence at Pavlovsk, were the scenes of frequent concerts at which quartets were played with Wieniawski as first violinist. In 1862 the Prince assumed the governorship of the Polish Kingdom and left for Warsaw.

In 1862, Petersburg saw the opening of the conservatory, under the directorship of Anton Rubinstein. Wieniawski had been working voluntarily for the Russian Musical Society[32] for a year when he was offered the job of guidance of the violin class. The lecturers in the class were violinists of the imperial theaters: Alexander Terayevich of Vilnius, and Vienna-born Johann Raab.[33]

In 1865, three violinists graduated from Wieniawski's class, the first ever to receive complete musical education in Russia: Dmitry Panov (a violinist of the orchestra of the imperial theaters and later assistant to Leopold Auer), Konstanty Pushilov (also a violinist of the orchestra of the imperial theaters), and Vasily Salin. The list of Wieniawski's students includes the names of the well-known Ippolit Altani (a graduate from Professor Zaremba's class of 1866); Tatiana Barkan (silver medal winner in 1872 after completion of her studies under the direction of Professor Auer); Vasily Bessel, the founder of a well-known Petersburg publishing firm (a graduate from Professor Weikman's viola class of 1865); and Piotr Krasnokutski, another violinist of the imperial theaters and later a professor of the Petersburg Conservatory (a student of Professor Auer's who finished his studies in 1870).[34]

"He worked very hard during the first hour," writes Bessel, "and then his strength and energy began declining rapidly so that after the third hour he was really through. The three-hour long class took place twice a week. That made six hours for 12 students, half an hour for each of them, the usual length in those days.

"He was not a very gifted teacher. Nevertheless, he was always a great artist: exuberant, quick-tempered, charming, irresistible, a little bit careless, sometimes furious."[35]

Torn between foreign and domestic concert tours and teaching duties, Wieniawski decided to leave the conservatory in 1868. His class was taken over by Leopold Auer.

Henryk's elder brother Julian Wieniawski, who had been an insurgent in the January 1863 Uprising, had to join the wave of political refugees who sought shelter in France and Germany. Julian found himself pardoned under the amnesty, owing to his famous brother's entreaties at the Tsar's court.

Attached to Petersburg as the Tsar's subject and employee, Henryk devoted his several-month-long leave to foreign travel and concert tours. On such occasions, Mr. and Mrs. Wieniawski left their two children with Henryk's parents in Lublin. The itinerary of their Western European voyages always included Mrs. Wieniawski's native London. In 1861, Henryk played a concert there with Nicolai Rubinstein.

During the spring and summer of 1863 the virtuoso toured

Pavlovsk.

Four members of the St. Petersburg Conservatory faculty: *Above, left:* Karol Schubert (double-bass); *Above, right:* Karol Davidov (double-bass and music history); *Below, left:* Henrietta Nissen-Saloman (voice); *Below, right:* Leopold Auer (violin).

Julian Wieniawski, Henryk's older brother.

A list of Henryk's pupils at the St. Petersburg Conservatory.

II. СКРИПКА.

Профессоръ Венявскій

Воспитанники:

95. Абаевъ.
96. Альтани.
97. Баранецкій.
98. Бессель.
99. Бѣловъ.
100. Вороновъ.
101. Гудаловъ.
102. Пушиловъ.
103. Фейтъ.

Revue et Gazette Musicale, May 13, 1866.[xxvi]

.ˑ. *Saint-Pétersbourg.* —On applaudit ici en ce moment Mlle Couqui, la charmante danseuse qui a été si fêtée à Vienne. — Henri Wieniawski, le célèbre violoniste, a obtenu du czar une augmentation d'appointements de 1,000 roubles argent, en sa qualité de violon-solo de Sa Majesté, et de plus un congé de cinq mois. — Ant. Rubinstein a donné deux brillants concerts à Moscou. — *La Belle Hélène* est jouée trois fois par semaine au théâtre français.

Henryk Wieniawski.

The Musical Times, **June 1, 1861.**

Mr. Santley, and Herr Formes, were also effective in their several parts.

The Friday Opera Concerts have been well attended. The performers upon these occasions have included Madame Grisi, Madlle. Titiens, Madame Miolan Carvalho, Madame Alboni, Signor Giuglini, Signor Belletti, Mr. Ole Bull, Wieniawski, &c. There have also been exhibitions of flowers, and various concerts, at which other artists have sung, including Miss Emily Spiller, Miss Mackenzie, Miss E. Wilkinson, Messrs. Cooper, Thomas, and others, with the National Choral Society, the Swiss singers, the Christy's Minstrels, &c.

Nicolai Rubinstein.

Joachim, Ernst, and Wieniawski.

London.

St. Petersburg.

A concert of Henryk Wieniawski
in the salon of the Grand Prince
Konstanty. At the piano is
Aleksander Dreyschock; on the
right is the Grand Prince.

Amsterdam, Copenhagen, Liège and paid a routine visit to Rhineland's resorts, the favorite rendezvous of the flower of society and well-known artists, and famous not only for their beautiful landscapes and medicinal waters but also as gambling centers. Wieniawski, an inveterate gambler, often played all his money away. No matter how much money he earned for recitals and concerts, he often found himself penniless.

During concert seasons (May through June) Wieniawski frequently played at the famous Musical Union Matinées in London. In 1866, he presented his "Fantasy on themes from *Faust*," Op. 20, which received rave reviews.

In winter, 1866, Wieniawski played in Romania. He could never have expected that his appearance on February 1st might be used as the smoke-screen for a coup. "The night Wieniawski was performing in the capital, Prince Cuza was forced to abdicate. As Bucarest aristocrats were listening to the Polish virtuoso playing, a handful of rebellious officers gathered at a top secret meeting in the same building and decided to strike. Naturally, the timing of the recital was intended to mislead the Prince and facilitate the surprise attack."[36]

"The tour of Sweden, Norway, and Denmark was another fascinating experience. Ovations, distinctions, and honors welcomed him everywhere. The Academy of Fine Arts in Stockholm granted Wieniawski membership, and the King conferred the Vasa Order on him. Some students unharnessed the horses of his carriage and carried the artist through the exultant crowd to the hotel. In Oslo, the aged Ole Bull sent him a letter asking for a meeting. The hotel's owner, proud of receiving the two virtuosos, treated them to a lavish breakfast.

A caricature of a concert given by Wieniawski.

"In Denmark, whose audiences were particularly generous with ovation, the artist was decorated with the Order of Daneborg."[37]

After the Scandinavian triumph, Wieniawski arrived in Paris again. A group of old friends gave him a warm welcome. Even Berlioz, respectful of his reputation as Massart's favorite student, committed their past quarrel to oblivion. Wieniawski appeared then at the great World's Fair, which opened in 1867. In June, in the Théâtre Italien, he played an excellent concert with Alfred Jaëll which was widely acclaimed in the press.

The Petersburg routine was conducive both to improvement of Wieniawski's masterly technique and to the writing of new compositions. It was there that the artist completed his Concerto no. 2 in D minor, Op. 22, which received enthusiastic praise among the critics.

In early summer 1869, the maestro was received at the court of Sultan Abdulazis in Constantinople.

In April, 1870, Wieniawski made his first Warsaw appearance in ten years. "The first night drew only 473 people to the Grand Theater house. However, the next concert was attended by an au-

Amsterdam.

Copenhagen.

Revue et Gazette Musicale, July
12, 1863.XXVII

.*. Un festival qui a duré plusieurs jours vient d'avoir lieu à Liége.
La musique n'y avait point été oubliée, et le directeur du Conservatoire,
M. Soubre. a donné en cette occasion une preuve de sa capacité ; car il
a organisé dans le délai d'un mois à peine un concert qui offrait de
sérieuses difficultés à vaincre et qui a parfaitement réussi. Haendel et
Mendelssohn en ont fait les frais. *La Fête d'Alexandre* et *Judas Machabée*
du premier ; la *Nuit de Walpurgis* du second, ont profondément remué
l'auditoire. Des artistes distingués avaient été appelés à Liége pour cette
solennité. Henri Wieniawski, premier violon solo des théâtres de Russie, a
joué trois morceaux, dont un concerto de Mendelssohn et un air varié de
sa composition fort remarquable, avec une pureté, un fini, une beauté
de son qui ont excité un véritable enthousiasme. Mme Charton-Demeur
a chanté avec autant de style que de sentiment l'air d'*Alceste* et celui du
Freischütz. Jourdan et Stockhausen ont brillamment concouru au succès,
dont M. Soubre peut également revendiquer sa bonne part.

Ems.

Homburg.

A loss at the roulette table.

An advertisement for Wieniawski's 1866 London engagement.

Revue et Gazette Musicale, June 3, 1866. xxviii

Two manuscript pages of the score of Wienlawski's "Fantasy on themes from *Faust*."

Ole Bull.

Stockholm.

Oslo.

Wieniawski's opp. 19 and 20.

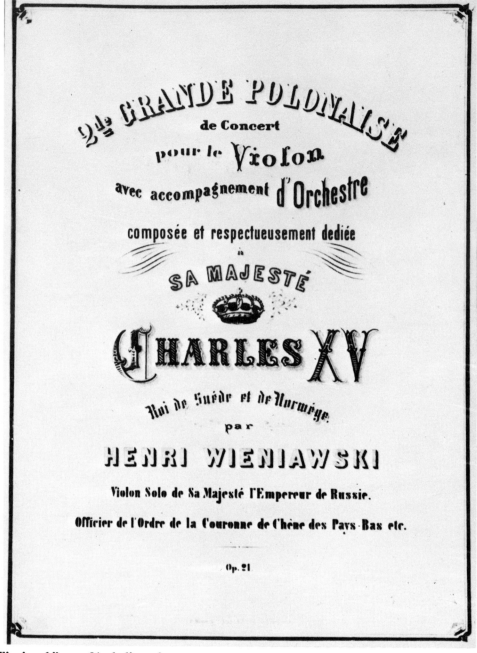

Wieniawski's op. 21, dedicated to
Charles XV, King of Sweden and
Norway.

The Paris World's Fair.

Pablo de Sarasate.

The first page of the manuscript of the score of Wieniawski's Violin Concerto no. 2, op. 22.

Wieniawski's op. 22, dedicated to Sarasate.

Allo. mod.to 2.d Concerto

Henri Wieniawski, op. 22.

Constantinople.

Henryk Wieniawski.

Jozef Wieniawski.

The Polish actress Helena Modrzejewska, a friend of the Wieniawskis.

dience of 1,300, who gave the artist a thunderous standing ovation. The delighted listeners turned towards the box in which his parents and wife were sitting and applauded in their honor."[38]

The third recital was on May 7. This time Henryk was accompanied by Jozef, in the hall where the brothers had already played many years before. The audience, who saw the two consummate artists onstage together again, well remembered the last performance of the "golden-haired boys."

In February, 1871, Wieniawski wrote the following to Antoni Door, his accompanist and piano teacher at the Vienna Conservatory: ". . .I have just returned from Helsingfors, where two concerts gave me quite unexpectedly over 1,800 roubles. I am very ill, with acute pharyngitis, and I do not think I will be able to work again very soon. I shall go to Vienna in March, if I am well enough by then. For the time being, there is nothing certain I can tell you save that my wife presented me twins as a New Year's gift!. . . Would you be so kind, my dear friend, to apologize on my behalf for the cancellation of my Vienna recitals. With heartfelt greetings, your colleague and father of four children—H. Wieniawski."[39]

Deeply upset by a painful incident at the home of Fiodor Berg, Wieniawski resigned his post in Petersburg. He could not stay any longer among people who demanded little less than servility on the one hand, and, on the other, did not know how to protect the artist against disrespect and arrogance. At this point, from Anton Rubinstein came a proposal to tour the United States of America.

"Wieniawski and Rubinstein had been promised the fee of 300,000 francs. Half of the money was to be deposited at a bank and the relevant agreement was concluded through the mediation of a Vienna solicitor, Dr. Jaques. The offer seemed very attractive then. In fact, however, the agreement left a large margin for the employer's arbitrary decisions."[40]

"There was not a single large town in which they did not receive a very enthusiastic welcome from the audiences. They often played two or even three recitals a day. The impresario insisted on strict and uncompromising observance of the contract. Wieniawski, normally quick to lose self-control and cancel his recitals in cases of slight indisposition, had to pull himself together, and in fact did so through a tremendous mobilization of self-discipline, in order to fulfill his obligations."[41] Despite the strain of having split with Rubinstein, he decided to extend his tour and went to San Francisco. He stayed there for nearly a year.

Near the end of 1874 he came to Brussels to work at the Conservatoire, where he had been asked to conduct quartet classes (created especially for him), and also violin classes, as a substitute for the ill Vieuxtemps. Wieniawski held the post of Professor at the Brussels Conservatoire until September, 1877.

"The effects of Wieniawski's pedagogical work in Brussels were outstanding. From San Francisco came Leopold Lichtenberg to

New York.

Henryk Wieniawski and his wife.

A later photograph of Henryk and Isabel.

Fyodor Berg (with his signature).

Revue et Gazette Musicale, **June 23, 1872.**[xxix]

*** Les impresarii américains Maurice Grau et Chizzola-Albitès étaient la semaine dernière à Paris, et y ont complété par plusieurs engagements le personnel d'artistes qui doivent accomplir la saison prochaine, sous leur direction, un voyage musical en Amérique. M. Grau dirigera une tournée de concerts aux Etats-Unis, à la Havane et au Canada; les artistes dont il s'est assuré le concours sont MM. Antoine Rubinstein, Henri Wieniawski, Mlle Liebhart (de Vienne), Mlle Orméni, contralto, et l'accompagnateur M. Rembielinski, qu'il vient d'engager. — M. Chizzola-Albitès a réuni une troupe d'opéra-bouffe dont *l'étoile* est Mlle Aimée; il jouera principalement les ouvrages d'Offenbach et de Lecocq, entre autres *la Princesse de Trébizonde* et *les Cent Vierges,* qu'il vient d'acquérir des éditeurs.

Revue et Gazette Musicale,
October 20, 1872.[xxx]

Revue et Gazette Musicale,
December 8, 1872.[xxxi]

Signale für die Musikalische Welt,
November 27, 1872.[xxxii]

Paulina Lucca.

Anton Rubinstein.

un village de l'Asie Mineure.

. *Baltimore.* — Rubinstein et Wieniawski continuent leurs triomphales pérégrinations à travers les villes de l'Union. Leurs concerts donnés à Baltimore, au théâtre de Ford, ont provoqué, comme partout, le plus grand enthousiasme.

. *Cincinnati.* — Le festival qui sera donné ici, au mois de mai, sous

Revue et Gazette Musicale,
January 19, 1873.[xxxiii]

Kellogg et un nouveau ténor, Verati, ont obtenu un brillant succès.

. *Baltimore.* — Rubinstein a donné le 28 mars son concert d'adieu. La grande tournée artistique qu'il a accomplie aux Etats-Unis, avec Henri Wieniawski, est arrivée à son terme, et les deux éminents virtuoses ne tarderont pas à faire voile pour l'Europe.

Revue et Gazette Musicale, May
4, 1873.[xxxiv]

San Francisco.

A carriage-ride through the
French countryside.

A concert in Brussels' Théâtre de
la Monnaie.

Henryk Wieniawski.

***Revue et Gazette Musicale**, June
8, 1873.[XXXV]

⁂ A son retour d'Amérique, — où il a donné en 240 jours 215 concerts, dont 50 à New-York, — Antoine Rubinstein a passé par Paris. Il
n'y est resté que la journée de jeudi dernier, et c'est le salon hospitalier
de M. et Mme Massart qui a profité du court séjour de ce prince du
piano. Rubinstein a joué, en petit comité d'artistes, quelques-unes des
douze charmantes *Miniatures* qu'il a dédiées à Mme Massart, une barca-
rolle et une grande valse-caprice qui est bien la chose la plus étonnante
du monde, comme gymnastique « digitigrade » et qu'il faut entendre et
voir exécuter au célèbre virtuose. Ce morceau — entre cent cinquante
autres — a révolutionné tout le public musical des États-Unis. Rubinstein,
du reste, en véritable artiste qu'il est, n'y attache pas d'autre importance
que celle d'un passe-temps musical. Le passe-temps, en tout cas, n'est
pas précisément à la portée de toutes les mains. — Rubinstein se rend
à Leipzig, et de là à Saint-Pétersbourg. Henri Wieniawski, qui a partagé
ses succès dans la tournée musicale d'Amérique, la continue pour son
propre compte dans les villes de l'ouest, avec l'impresario Grau.

⁂ Le Casino d'Enghien se prépare à faire son ouverture sous la
direction de M. Vachot, l'ancien impresario du théâtre de la Monnaie

***Revue et Gazette Musicale**,
December 20, 1874.[XXXVI]

de l'Opéra de Paris, qui chantera *Faust* et plusieurs ouvrages du reper-
toire de l'Opéra-Comique, *Martha* entre autres.—Henri Wieniawski, après
le succès qu'il a obtenu au concert populaire, s'est fait entendre dans
diverses réunions musicales : au Cercle artistique, à la Grande-Harmonie (premier concert de l'Association des artistes musiciens) ; partout il
a été fêté, acclamé, rappelé. A la Grande-Harmonie, les artistes lui ont
offert un archet d'honneur et une couronne.

Wieniawski (Henri)

né à Lublin (Russie) le 10 juin 1835.

nommé Concert-Meister professeur de violon et de quatuor 28 décembre 1874 5000 fr.

Démission acceptée le 27 7bre 1877

marié à le

à

né à le

le 1er avr. 1880, à Moscou.

VIOLON.

Professeur : M. COLYNS.

Décembre 1875 : 8 élèves; 4 auditeurs.
» 1876 : 8 » 2 »

Moniteur : M. *Van Stynvoort*, 1er prix en 1873.

Décembre 1875 : 8 élèves.
» 1876 : 8 »

Moniteur : M. *Hoyois*, 1er prix en 1875.

Décembre 1875 : 8 élèves.
» 1876 : 7 »

Moniteur : M. *Houben*, 1er prix en 1876.

Décembre 1876 : 7 élèves.

Professeur : M. WIENIAWSKI.

Décembre 1875 : 7 élèves; 1 auditeur.
» 1876 : en congé jusqu'au 1r octobre 1877.

Professeur-adjoint : M. A. Cornélis.

Décembre 1875 : 6 élèves.
» 1876 : 7 »

MARDI 3 AOUT 1875.

Audition des classes de quatuor (M. Henry Wieniawski).

I. Quatuor en *ut majeur* (no 9) . . . . . . BEETHOVEN.
exécuté par MM. Schnitzler, Cats, Kes, Bouman.

II. Étude no 6 . . . . RODE.
exécutée à l'unisson par tous les élèves de la classe.

III. Quatuor en *sol majeur* (no 1) . . . . . . MOZART.
exécuté par MM. Baudot, Vanden Broeck, Dabsalmont, Arnouts.

Violon : M. Léopold Lichtenberg (*avec grande distinction*), de San-Francisco (Californie), 14 ans, et M. Ed. Heimendahl, d'Elberfeld (Prusse), 18 ans (élèves de M. Wieniawski); M. Charles Houben, d'Anvers, 20 ans (élève de M. Colyns).
Piano (M. Brassin) : M. Jabez Streeter, de Littlehampton (Angleterre), 21 ans; M. Gust. Kefer, de Jambes, 21 ans.

Documents and records from Wieniawski's tenure at the Brussels Conservatory.[xxxvii, xxxviii, xxxix, xl]

François-Auguste Gevaert, director of the Brussels Conservatory.

Protocol for the 1876 session of the Conservatory Violin Competition.

Tony Binder's drawing of Wieniawski.

HENRI WIENIAWSKI

24 rue de Florence Avenue Louise Bruxelles.

A rare calling-card with Wieniawski's Brussels address written in his own hand (courtesy of Dr. Herbert R. Axelrod).

veaux directeurs, MM. Stoumon et Calabresi. — Le deuxième et dernier concert du Conservatoire a eu lieu dimanche dernier, sous la direction de M. Gevaert ; il a fort bien réussi. Henri Wieniawski, Brassin, Aug. Dupont, Joseph Servais, des maîtres dont l'Ecole est fière, s'étaient chargés des soli instrumentaux et ont puissamment aidé au succès.

** *Vienne*. — La représentation au bénéfice de Mme Patti, à l'Opéra-

Revue et Gazette Musicale, May 9, 1875.[xli]

Karol Gregorowicz.

Arma Senkrach.

study with him; among his most gifted students were: Izydor Schnitzler, Karol Gregorowicz, and an American, Arma Senkrach; two others (Heimendahl and Katz) succeeded in winning first place awards. Eugène Ysaÿe was Wieniawski's private student. Wieniawski found the most sincere friends in Gevaert's family; an outstanding pianist and teacher at the Brussels Conservatory, Louis Brassin, arranged there evenings of collective music, devoted to chamber music, the so-called Union Instrumentale."[42]

With the beginning of 1875 he gave concerts in Paris—"his talent still seems to deserve the greatest admiration." The critic's reservations following the popular concert, refer to the interpretation of the music: "The performance of the *Romance* (by Beethoven) would have been very good, if it had not been for the few caprices of style, concessions made by the master to the audience, which we could do without."[43] His concerts in Paris were interrupted by a visit to Holland, but on March 21, *Revue et Gazette Musicale* again reported from Paris: "Henryk Wieniawski, after his return from the musical tour of Holland and northern France, performed, accompanied by orchestra, Mendelssohn's Concerto in E minor, at the Henri Herz Hall last Wednesday."

Later, residing and working continually in Brussels, he made frequent concert excursions to London, Spaa, Gandave, Manchester.

He spent the winter of 1875/76 in Poland. In January, together with his brother, Wieniawski gave three concerts in Warsaw.

And later, Paris again. Performance at the Conservatoire: an excellent performance of Beethoven's Violin Concerto. He played it, according to the critic, "with the precision of a machine, with the breadth of tone and beautiful singing quality which make him one of the most outstanding talents." However, amidst the raptures of admiration there are always words of reproof: "This outstanding interpretation. . .left only more seriousness of expression to be desired. In a piece of this type, the master should completely forget about the audience, so that he would not be tempted to make concessions to it. And in the end the applause and the encores would not be less generous than those last Sunday."[44]

Concerts at the Théâtre Italien, Théâtre Ventadour, and Opéra Comique, came next. Lavish applause for the violinist of "a great school." In the Autumn—London. And again, as everywhere else, a great success.

"At the fifth concert of the Crystal Palace, Wieniawski attained a great success, playing Beethoven's Violin Concerto," wrote one critic, who added: "The artist intends to set out for a concert tour of the continent which will include Vienna, Graz, Prague, Pest, etc."[45]

"In November of 1876 Wieniawski gave concerts at the Musik-Verein Hall in Vienna. At first the attendance was poor, due to the fact that at that very time, simultaneously with Wieniawski and in the posh surroundings of Bösendorfer Hall, Pablo Sarasate was

Eugène Ysaÿe.

Revue et Gazette Musicale,
January 3, 1875.[xlii]

Revue et Gazette Musicale,
February 7, 1875.[xliii]

Revue et Gazette Musicale, **July
11, 1875.**[xliv]

Wladyslaw Mierzwinski.

Teresa Titiens.

⁎ A signaler encore les concerts ou représentations donnés dans
le même but : — A Saint-Quentin, par la Société philharmonique de
cette ville, avec le concours de Mme Alard-Guérette, qui a été très-
applaudie dans l'arioso du *Prophète* et dans l'air des *Saisons* de V. Massé,
et du violoncelliste E. Dufour ; — à Lyon, où le directeur du Conservatoire, M. Ed. Mangin, a récolté en deux séances (un concert et un
salut solennel en musique) 23,400 francs ; — aux Eaux-Bonnes, par
M. Reuchsel et son orchestre ; — à Poitiers, par l'œuvre de Notre-Dame
des Dunes, avec le concours de MM. E. Lévêque, Robyns, Seghers et
Giraudet ; — à Bruxelles, par l'orchestre du théâtre de la Monnaie,
sous la direction dô M. Joseph Dupont ; — à Spa, où Gustave Nadaud et
Henri Wieniawski ont vaillamment payé de leurs personnes ; — à Pé-
rouse, par plusieurs artistes renommés en Italie, auxquels s'étaient

Revue et Gazette Musicale,
August 1, 1875.[xlv]

Anna Yesipova.

William Cusins.

Revue et Gazette Musicale,
August 1, 1875.[xlvi]

⁎ *Gand.* — Le festival des 25 et 26 juillet a fort bien réussi. Les
Saisons de Haydn, un chœur nouveau de M. Gevaert, *De Ontwaking* (le
Réveil), l'Ouverture jubilaire de Hanszens, la cantate *De Schelde* (*l'Es-
caut*), de M. Pierre Benoît, celle de M. Gevaert, *Jacob Van Artevelde*, y
ont été exécutés sous la direction de M. De Vos. Les soli vocaux et
instrumentaux étaient interprétés par Mlle Hamaekers, MM. Warot,
Blauwaert et Henri Wieniawski.

In the Saski Gardens.

Revue et Gazette Musicale, April 2, 1876.[xlvii]

.*. Le violon de Wieniawski sur la scène des Italiens et Vieuxtemps conduisant l'orchestre : il y avait là assurément de quoi attirer et passionner les amateurs. Aussi la salle Ventadour était-elle en fête mardi dernier ; mais le public eût été plus nombreux encore si l'on avait annoncé plus longtemps à l'avance ce concert d'un si vif intérêt. Wieniawski était merveilleusement disposé ce soir-là : c'est dire que son jeu a été superbe, large et profondément senti. Le 5e concerto de Vieuxtemps, en *la* mineur, a été l'occasion d'une ovation méritée pour l'auteur et pour l'interprète. M. Wieniawski a aussi joué avec un style parfait, un son magnifique et un sentiment entraînant la romance en *fa* de Beethoven, une polonaise de sa composition et ses variations sur des airs russes : on était heureux d'applaudir le violoniste de grande école que ses sympathies pour le public parisien nous ramènent de temps à autre, mais pas assez souvent à notre gré. — Mme Engalli a chanté avec beaucoup d'ampleur l'arioso du *Prophète*, un air de *Charles VI* et le brindisi de *Lucrezia Borgia*; ce dernier morceau a été bissé.—Il est presque superflu de dire que l'orchestre, sous la direction magistrale de Henri Vieuxtemps, a marché à souhait, bien qu'on n'eût pu faire qu'une répétition.

Henryk Wieniawski.

A view of Brussels.

A Viennese tavern-garden.

The contemporary Polish
composer Wladyslaw Zelenski.

*In Front of the Grand Theater in
Warsaw.*

beginning his triumphal march through Germany. However, the greatest competition for Wieniawski was performances of an opera singer, Christina Nilsson, which diverted the attention of all and were received with great enthusiasm. Ill and confined to his bed, Wieniawski cancelled his second concert and had to prolong his stay in Vienna more than he intended, as well as change the dates of his concerts in other towns.

"After returning to good health, he gave a series of concerts which the audiences found ravishing. Together with Louis Brassin, Wieniawski played at Bösendorfer Hall, where, in spite of the serious competition from Christina Nilsson, enthusiastic listeners thronged. 'Wieniawski played like a god' - wrote fascinated critics. He had to repeat the Polonaise in A major several times. He received a laurel wreath from his admirers at one of the concerts. A concert together with Christina Nilsson at Kroll Theater marked the climax of his success. The gate money from this concert was intended for the 'Concordia' society of newsmen. The enthusiasm of the listeners reached its peak when Braga's Serenade and Gounod's *Ave Maria* (voice, violin, piano) followed the artists' solo performance. Wieniawski stayed in Vienna all through the January of 1877. After each 'farewell' concert there was always another, and each time Bösendorfer Hall was full. Budapest concerts planned for the beginning of January, where Wieniawski was to play together with Alfred Grünfeld, had to be rescheduled for the end of February to leave time for a tour of Malopolska's towns."[46]

"From Vienna, where. . .Wieniawski's concerts were received with unanimous appreciation, he left for Prague and there was taken seriously ill. Fortunately his illness did not last long. He recovered quickly and, continuing his artistic tour, made his way towards the motherland, to recapture the sympathies of his countrymen with his unmatched playing."[47]

In February of 1877 Wieniawski came to Lwow, where he gave four concerts, the last one (as was customary for Wieniawski) for charity. In the intervals between the concerts he visited several provincial towns (among others Stanislawow, Czerniowce); his next concerts were cancelled due to his illness, which confined him to his bed. "Wieniawski's last concert," wrote one of Lwow's papers,[48] "as we have announced earlier, took place last Saturday (i.e., the 17th of this month). The performer was greatly wearied by constant journeys, and even felt weak on the day of the performance. If it had been a matter of his own profits, he would have surely called off the performance and would have used that time for rest, the more so because there was a new journey awaiting, and on the next day a concert in Cracow, which had been announced a week before. But Wieniawski was to play for charitable purposes, and that is why he did not hesitate even one moment."

By way of Tarnow—where he also performed—Wieniawski went to Cracow. There he gave a wonderful concert, accompanied at the

A public billiard academy in Paris.

Cracow.

Prague.

158

Lwow.

piano by a brilliant accompanist, who would later be a famous conductor, Arthur Nikisch. Finally, at the end of February, Wieniawski left for Budapest to give the long-awaited concerts there.

"At that very time, Franz Liszt, who from 1875 had been appointed president of the Hungarian Music Academy, stayed there each year from Christmas-time until Easter. Wieniawski's first steps led to Liszt, whom he adored and considered his master. On February 25, Liszt gave a magnificent dinner party to honor his guest. It was a touching scene, when the snow-white and raven-black hair of the two virtuosos tangled in the embrace, their external appearance being so in contrast: ascetic, thin, and short Liszt with plump and athletic Wieniawski at his side.

"The first concert in Budapest took place on February 27, 1875, in the small Redoubt Hall (Sala Redutowa) with the participation of a singer of the German opera house in New York, Luiza Lichtmay. Four days later, Wieniawski played for the second time before the amazed Hungarian audience, leaving a 'memorable impression,' and driving his audience into a state of ecstasy. He was admired for his unbelievable technique, wild temperament, and youthful fervor, so much in contrast with his heavy appearance."[49]

After the Budapest success, in April of 1877 Wieniawski gave concerts in the towns of Transylvania: Temesvár, Arad, Grosswardein. Everywhere he played the same program: the first part of Mendelssohn's Concerto, his own "Fantasy on themes from *Faust*" and the *Legend*, finishing with the then-popular *Hungarian Songs* of H.W. Ernst. The critics surpassed each other in praise. Nevertheless, he did not play in Klausenberg, the largest town of Transylvania, despite the fact that it had been planned. "We are grieved," wrote one of the daily papers, "that we will not be able to share in the delightful playing of Wieniawski; on the other hand, however, we cannot demand from the directors of the theater to provide our music lovers with this pleasure at such a high price."[50]

From Transylvania, Wieniawski went on a tour of southern Russia, the country "about which he said with admiration, that it was an ideal country for violinists and that it was there that should have been the motherland of violin playing."[51]

In October of 1877, after leaving the Brussels Conservatoire, Wieniawski played in Copenhagen, and during the next year visited London twice.

During that time "his heart disease was progressing at an alarming pace; the first attack and nervous shock following a brutal scene at the home of Count Berg, were not without consequence. Extremely obese, Wieniawski could not stand before the audience, but sat all through the performance; it shows how exhausted he was."[52]

In September of 1878 he was in Paris and participated in four concerts of Russian music, arranged and conducted by Nicolai Rubinstein. He was the "hero of the day" in all of them.

Franz Liszt.

The Redoubt Hall in Budapest.

Simbirsk.

Voronezh.

**Amalienborg Square in
Copenhagen.**

Mist in the Streets of London.

Henryk Wieniawski.

Later in the autumn of the same year, Wieniawski made a concert tour of Germany. Among other places, in November Wieniawski performed several times at the Kroll Theater in Berlin. On the first of these concerts, he suddenly fainted and lost consciousness. Joseph Joachim, who was present at the concert, and who had been for several years director of the Hochschule für Musik, replaced Wieniawski, apologizing to the audience that "he shall not be able to play the beautiful concerto of his dear friend (the planned program was Wieniawski's Concerto no. 2 in D minor, op. 22), but shall play Bach's Chaconne."[53]

Joseph Joachim.

Near the end of 1878—despite the catastrophic state of his health—Wieniawski went on a new grand concert tour of Russia. He was accompanied by the Parisian opera prima donna, Désirée Artôt-Padilla. Then, near the end of 1879, at the invitation of the director of the Moscow Conservatory (Nicolai Rubinstein), Wieniawski participated in a concert of the Moscow Music Society. From there—continuing his interrupted tour—the artist went to southern Russia.

"He had no sooner come to Kharkov than he had to go back to Moscow and seek Rubinstein's help. He, who by way of honoraria collected vast sums of money, was left penniless because of gambling and recklessness! He, in fact, had a life insurance for 200,000 francs, but, due to lack of money, fell into arrears with payments to the Insurance Society; the deadline of the payment was drawing near—a few days more and all of the insurance money would have been lost. Guided by a feeling of distress, Jozef Wieniawski came to Moscow as soon as he could, and almost simultaneously with him came Anton Rubinstein from Petersburg, after learning that his old friend was gravely ill. Jozef Wieniawski together with Nicolai Rubinstein arranged a symphony concert which brought in 3,000 rubles and saved the insurance money. Also, the Imperial Music Society in Petersburg, remembering Henryk Wieniawski's contribution, arranged a concert which brought 2,500 rubles. Wieniawski's heart disease progressed rapidly. He was put in St. Mary's Hospital in Moscow and under the supervision of doctor Zakharin. . .near the end of February 1880 his condition improved. Mrs. Nadiezhda von Meck, widow of the Landwarowsk-Romensk railroad founder, as well as patroness of Piotr Tchaikovsky, though personally unknown to Wieniawski, received him in her palace on Rozhdestvensky Boulevard. . .The utmost delicacy and solicitous care on the part of this idealist and also on the part of the pianist and composer Henryk Pachulski, were a comfort for the dying man in his last moments of life."[54]

Moscow's Great Bell.

Nikolai Rubinstein.

Jozef Wieniawski.

Anton Rubinstein.

Bolesnym faktem kończymy tę kronikę. *Henryk Wieniawski*, jeden z największych wirtuozów gry skrzypcowej, zakończył życie w Moskwie dnia 31 Marca r. b. Wieniawski był skrzypkiem fenomenalnym; nadzwyczajna technika łączyła się w nim z uczuciem, szlachetnym stylem i wysokim smakiem. Był on wychowańcem szkoły francuzkiej, uczniem Massart'a. Przez 12 lat piastował godność solisty dworu Petersburgskiego, a naostatku był professorem w Konserwatoryum Bruxelskiem. Choroba sercowa przecięła pasmo dni jego zbyt wcześnie, bo w 45 roku życia.

Henryk Wieniawski, shortly before his death.

List of Works
(for violin and piano unless otherwise noted)

PUBLISHED

Grand caprice fantastique, 1847 (Paris, c 1850)—**op. 1**
Allegro de sonate, 1848 (Leipzig, 1851), collab. J. Wieniawski—**op. 2**
Souvenir de Posen, mazurka (Kalisz, 1854)—**op. 3**
Polonaise no. 1, D, vn, orch (Brunswick, 1853)—**op. 4**
Adagio élégiaque, A (Brunswick, 1853)—**op. 5**
Souvenir de Moscou, vn, orch (Brunswick, 1853)—**op. 6**
Capriccio-valse, E, 1852 (Leipzig, 1854)—**op. 7**
Grand duo polonais (Berlin, 1855), collab. J. Wieniawski—**op. 8**
Romance sans paroles et Rondo élégant (Leipzig, 1853)—**op. 9**
L'école moderne, 10 études, vn (Bonn, 1854)—**op. 10**
Le carnaval russe (Leipzig, 1854)—**op. 11**
Two Mazurkas (Leipzig, 1853): 1. La champetre, 2. Chanson polonaise—**op. 12**
Fantaisie pastorale (? Leipzig, c 1863), lost—**op. 13**
Vn Conc. no. 1. f-sharp (Leipzig, 1853)—**op. 14**
Thème original varié (Leipzig, 1854)—**op. 15**
Scherzo-tarantelle, g (Leipzig, 1856)—**op. 16**
Légende, vn, orch (Leipzig, c 1860)—**op. 17**
[8] Etudes-caprices, vn, vn 2 acc. (Leipzig, 1863)—**op. 18**
Two Mazurkas, c 1860 (Mainz, 1870): 1. Obertass, 2. Le ménétrier—**op. 19**
Fantaisie brillante, on themes from Gounod's *Faust*, vn, orch (Leipzig, 1868)
—**op. 20**
Polonaise brillante no. 2, A, vn, orch (Mainz, 1870)—**op. 21**
Vn Conc. no. 2, d, 1862 (Mainz, 1870)—**op. 22**
Gigue, e, pubd posth.—**op. 23**
Fantaisie orientale, pubd posth.—**op. 24**

Without opus number: Kujawiak, a (Leipzig, c 1853), Kujawiak, C (Kalisz, 1853), Rozumiem [I have understood], 1v, pf (Poznan c 1855), Reminiscences of San Francisco (San Francisco, c 1874), Rêverie, f-sharp, va, pf (Leipzig, 1885), Cadenza to Viotti Vn Concs. nos 17 and 22 (New York, 1904).

UNPUBLISHED

Pre-1850: Aria and Variations, E; Fantasia and Variations, E; Nocturne, vn solo; Romance; Rondo alla polacca, e; Variations on an Original Mazurka.

c1850-51: Duet on Finnish themes, 3 duos concertants, collab. J. Wieniawski; Fantasia on a theme from Meyerbeer's *Le prophète*; Fantasia on a theme from Grétry's *Richard coeur de lion*; March; 2 Mazurkas; Variations on "Jechal Kozak zza Dunaju"; Variations on the Russian National Anthem.

Post-1851: Cadenza to Beethoven Vn Conc., 1854, lost; Fantasia on a theme from Bellini's *La sonnambula*, c1855; Souvenir de Lublin, concert polka, c1855.

Notes to Text

[1]According to the birth certificate of Tadeusz Wieniawski himself; also in birth certificates of his sons (Henryk, Józef, and Alexander): "Master of Medicine, Surgery, Midwifery, and Philosophy."

[2]Information obtained from Wieniawski's grandson, Sir Brian Dean Paul.

[3]Julian Wieniawski, *Kartki z mego pamiętnika* (Warsaw: 1911), vol. 1, p. 10.

[4]A. Groza, *Mozaika kontraktowa. Pamiętnik z roku 1851* (Vilnius: 1857), p. 112., and R. Schwarz, "O Józefie Wieniawskim" in *Przeglad Muzyczny* (1877), no. 1, p. 25.

[5]*Revue et Gazette Musicale*, April, 1849.

[6]Józef Wladyslaw Reiss, *Henryk Wieniawski* (Cracow: 1963), p. 43.

[7]Ibid., p. 44.

[8]Ibid., p. 48.

[9]June 11, 1852.

[10]To the same addressee, May 29, 1852.

[11]April 10, 1853.

[12]Op.cit., p. 54.

[13]*Revue et Gazette Musicale*, March 5, 1854.

[14]Op.cit., p. 58.

[15]*Revue et Gazette Musicale*, May 7, 1854.

[16]July 9, 1854.

[17]Op.cit., p. 58.

[18]Ibid.

[19]Cf., A. Szyperski, *Henryk Wieniawski w Szczawnie Zdroju* (Szczawno: 1966), p. 3.

[20]J.W. Reiss, pp. 63-64.

[21]May 16, 1857.

[22]J.W. Reiss, p. 68.

[23]*Revue et Gazette Musicale*, November 14, 1858.

[24]J.W Reiss, pp. 71-72.

[25]Ibid., pp. 84-85.

[26]Cited after J.W. Reiss., p. 72.

[27]May 1, 1880.

[28]*Revue et Gazette Musicale*, April 29, 1860.

[29]Cited after J.W. Reiss, p. 76.

[30]Ibid., pp. 76-77.

[31]J.W. Reiss., p. 78.

[32]A.G. Rubinstein, *Avtobiograficheskie Vospominania* (Petersburg: 1889), p. 79.

[33]Information obtained from Tatiana Dmitrovna, director of the Study of History of Music at the Rimski-Korsakov Conservatory in Leningrad. Compare also: A.C. Ginsburg, "Gienrik Wieniawski v Rosii" in *Russko-polskie muzikalnie sviazi* (Moscow: 1963), p. 256-281.

[34]*Otchot Imperatorskiego Russkogo Muzikalnogo Obshchestva* (Petersburg: 1862-69).

[35]From the memoirs of V. Bessel about H. Wieniawski. Cited after N.F. Findeisen, *Vasilii Vasiliewich Bessel* (Petersburg: 1909), p. 182.

[36]Stefan Lakatos, "Wieniawski w Siedmiogrodzie" in *Muzyka* (1958), no. 4, p. 57.

[37]J.W. Reiss, p. 87.

[38]Ibid., pp. 88-89.

[39]Cited after J.W. Reiss, p. 90.

[40]J.W. Reiss, p. 93.

[41]J.W. Reiss, pp. 93-94.

[42]J.W. Reiss, p. 95.

[43]*Revue et Gazette Musicale*, January 10, 1875.

[44]*Revue et Gazette Musicale*, March 5, 1876.

[45]*Revue et Gazette Musicale*, November 5, 1876.

[46]J.W. Reiss, pp. 96-97.

[47]*Ruch Literacki*, January 1, 1877.

[48]*Tydzien literacki, Artystyczny, Naukowy i Spoleczny*, March 25, 1877.

[49]J.W. Reiss, op. cit., pp. 97-98.

[50]Cited after Stefan Lakatos, op. cit., p. 57.

[51]J.W. Reiss, p. 98.

[52]Ibid., p. 95.

[53]Cited after Zdzislaw Jahnke, "Koncert Wieniawskiego w Berlinie 1878 r." in *Ruch Muzyczny* (1948), no. 2, p. 23.

[54]J.W. Reiss, pp. 99-100.

Notes to Captions

[i]"Before going to Russia, where he is called by the Tsar's order, young Wieniawski, a twelve-year old violinist, Massart's pupil, will play on Sunday, January 30, at Mr. Sax's hall on 10 N.-St-Georges Street. The music world remembers the unprecedented success of this young virtuoso at the Conservatoire, where he had unanimously won the first place, thus being elevated above the others, almost all of whom were endowed with great talent. This fact itself should draw the attention of the audience to the young Wieniawski; the more surprising, therefore, are his compositions, which can compete with the works of mature artists. Henryk Wieniawski will play a concerto which won him the first prize in the competition, as well as an aria with variations and a capriccio of his own composition, with orchestral accompaniment. His young brother, an eight-year old pianist, pupil of Edouard Wolff, and also full of great promise, will be heard on this concert."

[ii]"[Petersburg]. . .we cannot, however, end our letter without saying a few words about young Wieniawski, the twelve-year old child, who won the first prize at the Paris conservatoire. He has made a rapid progress; the maturity of his talent is astonishing; the sureness of his bow can be seen above all in staccato; but what astonishes the most at his age is the liveliness and verve of his performance; it shows a stroke of genius. . ."

[iii]"Before their departure to Russia, the two young virtuosos, Henryk and Józef Wieniawski, played at the St. Cecilia Hall in a concert given by Lady Sabatier-Gaveaux for the benefit of a certain young student. Henryk, the violinist, played Ernst's *Fantasies* on the themes from *Otello*, and Józef, the pianist, played Gottschalk's *Bananatree* and Liszt's *Lucia*. The two brothers played, before the above pieces, a great duet of their own composition based on a Russian folk melody. They shared the applause, to which they both had an equal right."

[iv]"Vienna.—. . .on April 8, the Wieniawski brothers gave their fifth and last morning performance. Henryk, as usual, with great talent played the first part of the violin concerto by Mendelssohn and Ernst's fantasia on *Le Pirate*. At the request of the audience, he repeated *Le Carnaval russe* and *Les Chants russes*. Thalberg's fantasia on *Norma* played by Józef was rewarded by enthusiastic applause from all of the audience."

[v]"Munich.—The concert given by the Wieniawski brothers at the Odéon Hall has been truly an event of exceptional quality. The enthusiasm of the numerous audience rose steadily; warm applause often interrupted the performance, and the virtuosos have been called out several times."

[vi]"On the 9th of this month, the Wieniawski brothers gave their second concert in Berlin. The audience numbered not less than 1600 people, and the two young virtuosos have been called out fifteen times during the performance."

[vii]"Berlin.—. . .it is the fourth evening that the Wieniawski brothers are playing here, and it will probably not be the last. . ."

[viii]"Munich, July 22.—Among the musical celebrities attracted by our Exhibition, those enjoying the most attention are Spohr, Lindpainter, Moscheles, Taubert, Gade, and the Wieniawski brothers. . ."

[ix]"The two brothers, Henryk and Józef Wieniawski, stayed in Munich for the duration of the Exhibition, giving two superb concerts there. Now they are at Ostend, whence they will go to Frankfurt, Leipzig (for the Gewandhaus concerts), Brussels, and Holland. Henryk has just published a work entitled *L'Ecole moderne*, etude-capriccios for solo violin, which is attaining great success."

[x]"Würzburg. – The Wieniawski brothers are playing concerts at this moment with the greatest success."

[xi]"Leipzig. – . . .The first concert of the Gewandhaus was conducted by Messrs. Rietz and David. Among others, there performed such artists as the singer Mme de Holdorp and the famous violinist H. Wieniawski, who was received with warm applause from the audience and forced to give several encores, especially after the famous fantasia of Paganini."

[xii]"Henryk Wieniawski, the famous violinist, is presently in Berlin. During his stay in Poland he gave a concert in Lublin, his home town. The money from the concert will be used to found an orphanage. The concert brought in 5000 florins, and the virtuoso attained great success playing many of his own compositions: a grand fantasia on *La Sonnambula*, a concert polka, and *Souvenirs de Lublin*, a romance with variations dedicated to the ladies of the town."

[xiii]"It was not Henryk Wieniawski, violinist, but his brother Józef, pianist, who gave a concert in Lublin, his home town, about which we wrote in the last number of our paper. Henryk Wieniawski is still in Brussels."

[xiv]"Wiesbaden. – . . .Henryk Wieniawski is here at this time, but we are not sure whether we shall have the pleasure of listening to him."

[xv]"The Hague. – . . .Henryk Wieniawski, here – as everywhere else – the hero of last year's concerts, is back in Holland for the whole season. Standing ovations are being prepared. . ."

[xvi]"My Dear Friend, I was looking forward to spending Friday evening at Your house, and trying out one of Your beautiful quintets; unfortunately we have a chamber concert on Sunday and tomorrow evening we are having a rehearsal at Jacquard's, because we cannot meet during the day. We will be playing a very difficult quartet of Rubinstein, and I am afraid that Friday evening, and Saturday and Sunday morning may not be enough to play it well. I hope You will not resent my refusal; I shall lose more because of it than You, for I shall be deprived of the chance to listen to Your music, the popularity of which is unquestionable. What is postponed is not lost, and therefore I hope to see You soon. Your devoted – Henryk Wieniawski."

[xvii]"London. – Jullien's concerts have a vast audience. The most numerous audience was attracted by two evenings entitled 'Mendelssohn's Night' and 'Beethoven's Night,' during which only the works of these two great masters were performed. The famous pianist Arabella Goddard and Henryk Wieniawski were heard and were received with great warmth."

[xviii]"In London Wieniawski is as successful when playing Mendelssohn as when playing his own compositions. This is what happened to him in a concert in which Wieniawski interpreted a quintet of the master in such a way, that he had the honor of a call-out."

[xix]"Homburg. – Wieniawski has given concerts here with great success. He purchased Bériot's favorite violin, made by Magini [sic], for 24,000 francs. In Ostend, he played with double-bassist Piattini and pianist Rubinstein; they were received with great enthusiasm. People say of Wieniawski that he will marry the niece of the composer Osborne."

[xx]"Ostend. – This year's bathing season was one of the most magnificent, not only because of the presence of important personages such as His Majesty King of Belgium, Her Imperial Highness the Grand Duchess Helen. . .etc., etc., but also due to the presence of famous musical celebrities such as Rubinstein, Piatti, Wieniawski, Haumann, Mr. and Mrs. de Blaes, Count von Steinlein, Mr. and Mrs. Léonard, Edward Wolff, the cellist Poorten, the Russian violinist Bezekir-

ski, the tenor Wicart; such was the constellation of artists summoned here to make themselves heard before our august guests. We do not even have to add that they carried out their task with the superiority which distinguishes them. The first concert at the Casino was so successful, that a second musical celebration of this type is being arranged, and Mr. Léonard was so taken with Wieniawski's playing that he has proposed to set up a quartet, in which we shall hear together with Wieniawski and Léonard, Bezekirski and Piatti. Unfortunately Wieniawski is ill in bed. He is engaged to a young Englishwoman. On her departure, the Grand Duchess Helen gave him a beautiful brooch and diamond earrings for his fiancée."

xxi"Ems.—The King of Holland graced by his presence the concert of double-bassist Piattini and violinist Wieniawski, bestowing on the former the 'Oak' order, and on the latter a signet ring with the king's monogram in diamonds."

xxii"Mr. Henryk Wieniawski, violinist, will settle soon in St. Petersburg in the capacity of first violinist to His Imperial Majesty."

xxiii"Henryk Wieniawski has not yet purchased the Maggini violin, for which the owner Bériot is asking 20,000 francs. The transaction was delayed until both artists arrive in Petersburg this winter, where they will attend a meeting of contemporary violinists. Also in attendance will be Vieuxtemps and Laub."

xxiv"London.—. . .The Schiller Festival at the Crystal Palace was a notable event, which lacked not even one thing. There were music, banquets, speeches, and a march with torches. The main musical piece of the concert was a cantata whose text was written by the able and elevated pen of Mr. Freiligrath, and whose music was written by Mr. Pauer, with all the talent characteristic of a consummate musician. Wieniawski played the only solo at the concert and was covered with bravos."

xxv"London.—The Popular Concerts given this year at Saint-James Hall have been particularly successful. During the last evening, attention was particularly drawn to Messrs. Ch. Hallé, Wieniawski, Patti, and Mrs. Lemmens-Scherrington."

xxvi"St. Petersburg.—. . .Henryk Wieniawski, the famous violinist, as the soloist of His Majesty, has received from the Tsar a salary-increase of 1,000 rubles in silver, and in addition a five month vacation. . ."

xxvii"(Liège). . .Henryk Wieniawski, the first violin-soloist of the Russian theaters, played three pieces—including a concerto by Mendelssohn and a truly remarkable aria with variations of his own composition—with a purity, a finish, a beauty of sound which aroused real enthusiasm. . ."

xxviii"(London). . .Wieniawski, the violinist par excellence, created a sensation with his fantasia on the themes from *Faust*, filled with difficulties, which seem child's play for Wieniawski."

xxix"The American impresarios Maurice Grau and Chizzola-Albitès stayed in Paris last week to conclude contracts and assemble artists who, under their direction, will go on a musical tour of America next season. Mr. Grau will lead the concert tour of the United States, Havana, and Canada; the artists who will participate in this tour are, Messrs. Anton Rubinstein, Henryk Wieniawski, Miss Liebhart (from Vienna), Miss Ormeni, contralto, and the accompanist Rembieliński, whom he has just engaged. . ."

xxx"New York.—During his first concert, which was an utmost success, Rubinstein played his Concerto in D minor, his own transcription of Beethoven's Turkish March from the *Ruins of Athens*, the *Symphonic Etudes of Schumann*, variations by Händel and the Rondo in A minor of Mozart; Henryk Wieniawski received fervent applause for his playing of Mendelssohn's concerto and his own *Legend*."

xxxi"New York.—Rubinstein and Wieniawski, who have just made a tour of towns in the interior of the country, are still, along with Mrs. Lucca, the heros of the day."

xxxii"It is on three world-renowned names that all the attention of New York is presently turned: Anton Rubinstein, Henryk Wieniawski, and 'last but not least' Paulina Lucca; to the lavish measure of fame and fortune attained in Europe, America has added even more lavish homages and gold.

"Rubinstein and Wieniawski, not counting excursions to Boston, Philadelphia, and Washington, have been playing at Steinway Hall since the end of September. . . .The two wonderful musicians have revolutionized what is called the cultivated American music world."

xxxiii"Baltimore. – Rubinstein and Wieniawski are continuing their triumphal tour through American towns. Their concerts in Baltimore at the Ford Theater were met, as everywhere, with the greatest enthusiasm."

xxxiv"Baltimore. – On March 28, Rubinstein gave his farewell concert. The great artistic tour of the United States, which he had made with Henryk Wieniawski, came to an end, and the two eminent virtuosos will not delay to set sail for Europe."

xxxv"Upon his return from America, where in 240 days he gave 215 concerts, 50 of them in New York, Anton Rubinstein passed through Paris. . .Henryk Wieniawski, who shared in his success in the musical tour of America, is continuing it on his own account in the towns of the West, with the impresario Grau."

xxxvi"Brussels. – . . .After his success at the Popular Concert, Henryk Wieniawski was heard in several musical gatherings: the Cercle Artistique, the Grande-Harmonie (the first concert of the Association of Musical Artists); everywhere, he was honoured, applauded and called out. At the Grande-Harmonie, he was presented with an honorary bow and a crown."

xxxvii"Wieniawski (Henryk) born, in Lublin (Russia) on June 10, 1835. He was appointed concertmaster, professor of violin and of quartet on December 28, 1874. 5000 francs. The resignation has been accepted on July 27, 1877. Died on April 1, 1880, in Moscow."

xxxviii". . .Professor: Mr. Wieniawski. December 1875: 7 pupils, 1 auditor. December 1876: on vacation until October 1, 1877."

xxxix"Violin: Mr. Léopold Lichtenberg (with great distinction) from San Francisco (California), 14 years old, and Mr. Ed. Heimendahl from Elberfeld (Prussia), 18 years of age (students of Mr. Wieniawski); Mr. Charles Houben from Antwerp, 20 years of age (student of Mr. Colyns)."

xl"Competition of 1876. Violin. Today, Monday, July 31, at 10 o'clock in the morning, at the Conservatoire, under the leadership of its director Mr. Gevaert, assembled, as follows: the Prince de Caraman-Chimay, F. Coenen, Cramer, Vivien, appointed to the jury of the violin competition. There were four competitors. After the tests were ended, the President submitted to vote the question of awarding the first prize. The unanimous answer was 'yes.' The first prize with great distinction was given unanimously to Mr. Lichtenberg. The first prize went to Messrs. Heinmendahl and Houben. Mr. Rousen received a special award. . ."

xli"Brussels. – . . .The second and last concert of the Conservatoire took place last Sunday under the direction of Mr. Gevaert; it was very successful. Henryk Wieniawski, Brassin, August Dupont, Joseph Servais – the masters of whom the school is proud – undertook to play instrumental solos, making a major contribution towards the success."

xlii"The honours of the Sunday popular concert went to Henryk Wieniawski. It seems that this famous violinist has gathered new strength on this long concert tour of America, which he ended a few months ago, and on which every virtuoso risks squandering and diminishing his talent. In beautiful and high style as well as with great technical perfection, he performed Vieuxtemps' Concerto no. 5 in A minor. But we were almost witness to the moment when he was going to lose hold of the reins, because never has the orchestra of the Popular Concerts accompanied a virtuoso so carelessly. Fortunately, Wieniawski is firm in the saddle, and he did not lose his poise for even one instant. He was warmly applauded and called out several times after the concert."

xliii"Mrs. Jessipow and Messrs. Wieniawski and Dawydow were still performing last Wednesday at the Musical Institute of Mr. and Mrs. Comettant, in the company of Mrs. Carvalho and of the tenor Wladyslaw Mierzwinski. It was a wonderful evening and one can imagine without difficulty the stormy applause bestowed on all these greatly talented artists, only one of whom would have been enough to make the evening interesting and successful. . ."

xliv"London. – The eighth and last concert of the old Philharmonic Society took place last Monday, under the baton of Mr. Cusins. Henryk Wieniawski and Miss Titiens were the soloists."

xlv". . .In Spaa, Gustav Nadaud and Henryk Wieniawski courageously fulfilled their duty" (giving a concert for the benefit of the victims of a flood)."

xlvi"Gandava. – The Festival of July 25th and 26th went very well. . .Vocal and instrumental solos were presented by Miss Hamaekers and Messrs. Warot, Blauwaert, and Henryk Wieniawski."

xlvii"Wieniawski's violin on the stage of the Italian Theatre and Vieuxtemps' conducting the orchestra – that was what could attract and thrill real music lovers. Ventadour Hall also celebrated a similar gala last Tuesday; but the audience would have been even more numerous, if this very interesting concert had been announced earlier. That evening Wieniawski was exceptionally well-disposed: it is enough to say that his performance was exquisite, of a wide range, and deeply felt. Vieuxtemps' Concerto no. 5 in A minor was the occasion for a well-deserved ovation for the composer as well as the performer. In addition, Mr. Wieniawski played in a perfect style Beethoven's *Romance* in F, a Polonaise of his own composition, and his variations on Russian themes. We were happy to applaud the violinist of high order, whose affection for the Parisian audience brings him back to us from time to time, but not as often as we would like. . ."

xlviii"It is with a sad fact that we end this newspaper. Henryk Wieniawski, one of the greatest violin virtuosos, finished with his life in Moscow, on March 31st of this year. Wieniawski was a phenomenal violinist; extraordinary technique was combined with feeling, noble style, and high taste. He was an alumnus of the French school, a student of Massart's. For twelve years he held the dignified post of first soloist at the Petersburg court, and in the end was a professor at the Brussels Conservatory. A heart attack cut the thread of his days too early, in the forty-fifth year of his life."

		DATE DUE		